CUPCAKES FROM THE **HEART**

CUPCAKES FROM THE HEART

SAMANTHA BLEARS

Ivy Press

First published in the UK in 2010
Ivy Press
210 High Street, Lewes
East Sussex BN7 2NS, UK
www.ivypress.co.uk

British Library Cataloguing-in-Publication Data
A catalogue record for this book is available from the British Library

ISBN: 978-1-907332-47-0

Ivy Press
This book was conceived, designed, and produced by Ivy Press

Creative Director Peter Bridgewater
Publishers Jason Hook / Jenny Manstead
Design & Art Direction Wayne Blades
Senior Editor Polita Anderson
Design Grade Design
Photographer Clive Streeter
Illustrator Nick Gibbons

Printed in China
Colour Origination by Ivy Press Reprographics.

10 9 8 7 6 5 4 3 2 1

All spoon measurements are level, and teaspoons are 5ml and
tablespoons 15ml. Unless otherwise stated, eggs are medium and
should all be free-range. Oven temperatures specified are for
convection ovens; temperatures for fan-assisted ovens should be
adjusted according to the manufacturer's instructions.

Sterilizing jars
To sterilize new or used screw-top jars, preheat the oven to
150°C/300°F/Gas Mark 2. Wash the jars and lids thoroughly,
then rinse and dry well. Stand the jars and lids on a baking
sheet and heat in the oven for at least 20 minutes.

Contents

Foreword

It all started with my children, Georgie and Henry. They had their hearts set on us having a stall at the school Halloween fair. That sort of thing has never really appealed, but I bit the bullet: an old-fashioned cake stand seemed like the easiest thing to do! Two hundred cupcakes and a lot of nerves later, I shakily set up my little stand and was astonished when we sold out. Almost immediately my phone started ringing. By word of mouth, mums from school started ordering cakes for their children's parties and eventually word spread to local delis and shops. First I panicked, but then I learned that my decorative sugar-paste cut-outs were my saving grace. I used heaps of flowers and butterflies to cover up any icing accidents or sunken cupcakes and my customers loved them. A swirl of buttercream embellished with pretty, delicate cut-outs and a sprinkle of edible glitter proved to be magic. I had found my style literally by accident.

I was soon baking up to six hundred cupcakes a week in my own kitchen. Every available work surface was heaving, and when I couldn't fit any more home deliveries into the boot of my car, I decided that my cupcakes and I needed to find a new home. I've lived all over the world but I'm a London girl at heart, so when a store became available on London's legendary King's Road, I felt like the decision had been made for me. As we were such a little start-up, I did everything by hand, from building the counter in the bakery to creating our own pink and green candy-striped 'LOVE' logo. The Love Bakery opened its doors in March 2009, and a year later it is flourishing. I have the most wonderful customers who have made it what it is today by inspiring me to bake up new ideas – a cup of tea and a chat with the people who visit the shop is still the highlight of my day!

This book isn't about how to bake perfect cupcakes. It's about trying to make the most beautiful, perfectly formed cupcakes YOU can. If your cupcakes don't turn out like the photos in this book, what's the worst that can happen? It's only cake, you can eat your mistakes. As long as you remember it's supposed to be fun and bake with Love, you can't go far wrong.

Samantha Blears

PROPRIETOR, LOVE BAKERY

www.lovebakerylondon.com

I keep my kitchen at home stocked with the basic ingredients for vanilla and chocolate cupcake bases, and cream cheese frosting – along with a big box of icing sugar. Then when it comes to baking, I can tart up my creations with any other ingredients I happen to have handy. Not so long ago, if you'd told me I could bake a dozen cupcakes as easily as knocking up a plate of scrambled eggs, I wouldn't have believed you, but it really is that easy. All you need to get going is a selection of simple ingredients. You'll still need to go shopping for some of the recipes in this collection, but a well-stocked store cupboard will get you a long way. Here's my basic checklist…

———➔

caster sugar

OFFEE

For the Store Cupboard

Unsalted butter
Semi-skimmed milk
Free-range eggs
Full-fat cream cheese
Mascarpone cheese
Buttermilk
Double cream

Self-raising flour
Plain flour
Baking powder
Bicarbonate of soda
Cocoa powder
Vegetable oil
White wine vinegar

Caster sugar
Icing sugar
Granulated sugar
Soft light brown sugar
White sugar-paste icing

A selection of jams
Lemon curd
Clear honey
Apples, strawberries,
blueberries and other
fresh fruit
Lemons & Limes

Dark chocolate
Candy melts®
Candied peel
Ground Cinnamon
Ground Ginger
Food colourings
Vanilla, mint, rose
and other extracts
Instant coffee
Earl Grey tea bags
Oreo® biscuits
Chocolate-coated coffee
beans
Edible glitter
Edible sprinkles
Fresh mint

cocoa powder

As well as basic ingredients, you'll need some basic kitchen equipment. Once you have the essentials, you can start adding templates, fruit corers and the like as you expand your repertoire – or you can just improvize with what you have. If you get the baking bug, you should definitely consider investing in some of the more expensive equipment on the list. I still have my original electric mixer in use at the Love Bakery and, when you're making batches of cupcakes on a regular basis, bigger items like this are worth their weight in gold.

12-hole muffin tin
Two 24-hole mini muffin tins
Muffin cases
Mini muffin cases
Three 4-hole Yorkshire pudding tins
Giant cupcake tin
Two 20cm ring mould tins
Baking sheet
Greaseproof paper
Wire rack
Storage tins

Large freestanding
electric mixer

Food processor
Electric hand whisk
Blender
Microwave oven

Measuring scales
Measuring spoons
Measuring jugs
Mixing bowls
Hand whisk

Fine sieve
Rolling pin
Chopping board

Small, sharp knife
Cutters in a variety
of shapes
Ice cream scoop, size 16
Spatula
Wooden spoon
Metal tablespoon

Metal skewer
Apple corer
Zester
Grater
Butter brush
Can opener

Saucepan and
heatproof bowl

Kitchen scissors

Medium piping bags and
large star piping nozzles

Lolly sticks
Cellophane
Ribbon
Doilies

Ring mould tin

Scales & weights

Hand whisk

Food processor

Wooden spoon

Love
Favourites

These recipes are not only delicious stand-alone cupcake flavours, they also provide foundations for many of the more complex cupcake ideas in this book. They are undeniably simple and easy to adapt, and once you've mastered how to make a basic vanilla or chocolate cupcake, for example, you'll be knocking out dozens before you know it. It's also a great place to start if, like me in the beginning, you aren't used to baking and you're building up your basic repertoire of skills and store of ingredients.

Vanilla Cupcakes

Let's start at the beginning with the very first cupcake I ever baked. I can guarantee that EVERYONE will love this easy but effective recipe for a classic vanilla cupcake. When I opened Love Bakery, in the first weeks it was the only flavour we offered, and it remains my bestseller by a clear mile. I promise that when you have this one perfected, you'll be able to cook up a batch with your eyes closed. Keep it simple and you can't go far wrong.

MAKES

12 cupcakes

EQUIPMENT

12-hole muffin tin
12 muffin cases
Freestanding electric mixer
Mixing bowl
Spatula
Ice cream scoop, size 16
Wire rack
Medium piping bag and large star piping nozzle
   or palette knife

FOR THE CAKES

125g unsalted butter, at room temperature
125g caster sugar
1½ tsp vanilla extract
2 eggs, at room temperature
125g self-raising flour
½ tsp baking powder
3 tbsp semi-skimmed milk

FOR THE FROSTING

125g unsalted butter, at room temperature
½ tsp vanilla extract
250g icing sugar, sifted
1 tbsp semi-skimmed milk

FOR THE LOVE (OPTIONAL)

Yellow edible dust and sugar-paste daisies
   (see pages 81 and 141) and leaves, or red
   coloured sugar or edible sprinkles, pink edible
   dust and sugar-paste leaves

To make the cakes

- Preheat the oven to 180°C/350°F/Gas Mark 4 and line the holes of the muffin tin with muffin cases.
- Add the butter, caster sugar and vanilla extract to the electric mixer and cream together for 7 minutes, or until light and fluffy.
- Add the eggs, one by one, and mix for 2 minutes.
- Mix the flour and baking powder together in a separate bowl, then add to the mixer and mix until incorporated. Add the milk and mix for a further minute.
- Use the ice cream scoop to divide the mixture evenly between the muffin cases. Bake for 25 minutes.
- Remove the baked cupcakes from the oven and immediately transfer to a wire rack. Leave to cool.

To make the frosting

- Cream the butter and vanilla extract together in the mixer for 2 minutes until light and fluffy.
- Add the icing sugar and milk and mix for a further 2 minutes until well blended.

To add the love

- Top the cupcakes with the frosting, either by piping or spreading with a palette knife (see page 51).
- If you like, sprinkle the frosting with a little yellow edible dust and top with a sugar-paste daisy and leaf. Alternatively, roll the edge of the cupcakes in red coloured sugar or edible sprinkles, sprinkle the top with pink edible dust and add a sugar-paste leaf.

Love Tip

You can try using fresh vanilla pods instead of vanilla extract for a really authentic vanilla flavour – most supermarkets now stock them. Take one vanilla pod, slit open down its length with a small, sharp knife and scrape out the seeds, then fold seeds into the frosting.

This is a classic example of how adding one lovely, bold fresh ingredient can completely alter the taste of a basic vanilla cupcake. The result is maximum flavour with minimum effort, which is why it's much loved by the bakers at Love. Our customers seem to like it too – it's always a sellout. This light and airy, summery cupcake is a way to build up your repertoire without being too ambitious.

Lemon Cupcakes

MAKES
12 cupcakes

EQUIPMENT
12-hole muffin tin
12 muffin cases
Zester or grater
Freestanding electric mixer
Mixing bowl
Spatula
Ice cream scoop, size 16
Wire rack
Medium piping bag and large star piping nozzle
  or palette knife

FOR THE CAKES
125g unsalted butter, at room temperature
125g caster sugar
1 tbsp grated lemon zest
2 eggs, at room temperature
125g self-raising flour
½ tsp baking powder
3 tbsp semi-skimmed milk

FOR THE FROSTING
125g unsalted butter, at room temperature
1 tsp grated lemon zest
½ tsp lemon extract
250g icing sugar, sifted
1 tbsp semi-skimmed milk
Yellow paste food colouring

FOR THE LOVE (OPTIONAL)
Sugar-paste roses, leaves, daisies and butterflies
  (see pages 81 and 141)

To make the cakes
- Preheat the oven to 180°C/350°F/Gas Mark 4 and line the holes of the muffin tin with muffin cases.
- Add the butter, caster sugar and lemon zest to the electric mixer and cream together for 7 minutes, or until light and fluffy.
- Add the eggs, one by one, and mix for 2 minutes.
- Mix the flour and baking powder together in a separate bowl, then add to the mixer and mix until incorporated. Add milk and mix for a further minute.
- Use the ice cream scoop to divide the mixture evenly between the muffin cases. Bake for 25 minutes.
- Remove the baked cupcakes from the oven and immediately transfer to a wire rack. Leave to cool.

To make the frosting
- Cream the butter and lemon zest and extract together in the mixer for 2 minutes until light and fluffy.
- Add the icing sugar, milk and a little yellow food colouring and mix for a further 2 minutes until well blended.

To add the love
- Top the cupcakes with the frosting, either by piping or spreading with a palette knife (see page 51).
- If you like, decorate with sugar-paste roses, leaves, daisies and butterflies.

Love Tips
Not everyone has a zester, and if you don't, the best way to zest the lemon is with the fine side of a regular grater. Just watch your fingers! For an extra lemony kick, try soaking granulated sugar in lemon juice – you want it crunchy, not drenched, so add a little at a time – and sprinkle over the top of your frosting. Ready-made sugar-paste roses are widely available, and can be bought from most specialist cookery shops, or online from www.sugarshack.co.uk or www.cakecraftworld.co.uk.

Rose Cupcakes

Rose extract is a bit like magic – its fragrant flavour will simply transform the classic cupcake mixture into something truly exotic and atmospheric in a dash. And quite literally a dash, since you only need to add a small amount of extract, but you can use a touch less or more depending on how floral-tasting you like your cakes and their frosting. For an easy decoration option, top each cupcake with a beautiful crystallized rose petal.

MAKES
12 cupcakes

EQUIPMENT
12-hole muffin tin
12 muffin cases
Freestanding electric mixer
Mixing bowl
Spatula
Ice cream scoop, size 16
Wire rack
Medium piping bag and large star piping nozzle
  or palette knife

FOR THE CAKES
125g unsalted butter, at room temperature
125g caster sugar
1½ tsp rose extract
2 eggs, at room temperature
125g self-raising flour
½ tsp baking powder
3 tbsp semi-skimmed milk

FOR THE FROSTING
40g unsalted butter, at room temperature
100g full-fat cream cheese
2 tsp rose extract or essence, to taste
250g icing sugar, sifted

FOR THE LOVE (OPTIONAL)
Sugar-paste roses, butterflies and daisies
  (see pages 81 and 141)
Silver edible balls
Silver edible glitter, for sprinkling

To make the cakes
• Preheat the oven to 180°C/350°F/Gas Mark 4 and line the holes of the muffin tin with muffin cases.
• Add the butter, caster sugar and rose extract to the electric mixer and cream together for 7 minutes, or until light and fluffy.
• Add the eggs, one by one, and mix for 2 minutes.
• Mix the flour and the baking powder together in a separate bowl, then add to the mixer and mix until incorporated. Add the milk and mix for a further minute.
• Use the ice cream scoop to divide the mixture evenly between the muffin cases. Bake for 25 minutes.
• Remove the baked cupcakes from the oven and immediately transfer to a wire rack. Leave to cool.

To make the frosting
• Cream the butter, cream cheese and rose extract or essence together in the mixer for 2 minutes.
• Add the icing sugar and mix for a further 2 minutes until well blended. Watch closely as the frosting must remain firm if you are going to pipe it. Chill in the refrigerator until ready to use.

To add the love
• Top the cupcakes with the frosting, either by piping or spreading with a palette knife (see page 51).
• If you like, decorate the cupcakes with sugar-paste roses, butterflies and daisies and scatter with edible silver balls. Sprinkle with silver edible glitter.

Love Tips
Alternatively, you could use any fresh rose petals, which are all edible, or rosehips make a gorgeous, purely decorative finishing touch. As with any fresh ingredients, make sure petals or hips are well rinsed and carefully patted dry before using on your cupcakes.

Sweeties

What began as a drawer in my kitchen at home eventually became a cupboard in the Love Bakery, crammed full of lovely bits and bobs that I can never bear to throw away. I'm a complete magpie, and my precious scraps of ribbon, vintage jewellery, cellophane and pages torn from magazines have formed the inspiration behind many cupcakes sold in the Bakery. I often use Moodboards to get all my ideas together – you can see examples on pages 66–67 and 134–135. Your personal Just-in-Case Cupboard is a repository for all the things you might use to make your cupcakes individual and beautiful. It's also a safe place to keep cut-outs, templates, decorations and recipe ideas.

Scraps of wrapping paper
Scraps of paper to use for inspiration
Old invitations

Props to be used as decorations
Vintage finds
Moodboards
Stationery

Fabric
Scraps of lace
Buttons
Ribbon

Corsages
Flowers
Sweeties
Fairy lights

Crockery
Old jars

Vintage jewellery

notebook

Just-in Case Cupboard

Candy Canes

Chocolate Cupcakes

Everyone loves chocolate and everyone loves cake – it's as simple as that. So combine the two and you'll have hit the jackpot! The secret weapon here is the buttermilk, which will keep your cakes super moist and super moreish. It also acts as a wonderful preservative, as the extra moisture will mean that the cupcakes won't dry out. However, I can't guarantee that you'll get the chance to judge this in practice, as in my house and the Bakery they are usually eaten up in a flash.

MAKES
12 cupcakes

EQUIPMENT
12-hole muffin tin
12 muffin cases
Freestanding electric mixer
Mixing bowl
Spatula
Ice cream scoop, size 16
Wire rack
Medium piping bag and large star piping nozzle
  or palette knife

FOR THE CAKES
60g unsalted butter, at room temperature
150g caster sugar
1 egg, at room temperature
20g cocoa powder, sifted
150g plain flour
140ml buttermilk
½ tsp bicarbonate of soda
1½ tsp white wine vinegar

FOR THE FROSTING
60g unsalted butter, at room temperature
125g icing sugar, sifted
50g cocoa powder, sifted
4 tbsp semi-skimmed milk

FOR THE LOVE (OPTIONAL)
Sugar-paste flowers and leaves
  (see pages 81 and 141)
Silver edible glitter

To make the cakes
- Preheat the oven to 180°C/350°F/Gas Mark 4 and line the holes of the muffin tin with muffin cases.
- Add the butter and caster sugar to the electric mixer and cream together for 7 minutes, or until light and fluffy.
- Add the egg and mix for 1 minute.
- Add the cocoa powder and stir in by hand, then mix with the mixer for 1 minute. Add the flour and buttermilk and mix for 2 minutes, and then add the bicarbonate of soda and vinegar and mix for 1 minute.
- Use the ice cream scoop to divide the mixture evenly between the muffin cases. Bake for 25 minutes.
- Remove the baked cupcakes from the oven and immediately transfer to a wire rack. Leave to cool.

To make the frosting
- Cream the butter and icing sugar together in the mixer for 2 minutes.
- Add the cocoa powder and mix in by hand, then add the milk and mix with the mixer for 2 minutes until well blended.

To add the love
- Top the cupcakes with the frosting, either by piping or spreading with a palette knife (see page 51).
- If you like, decorate the cupcakes with sugar-paste daisies and leaves. Sprinkle with silver edible glitter.

Love Tip
For a triple choc whammy, when your mixture is in the muffin cases, take a handful of chocolate chips and gently drop a pinch into each case before you pop the tin into the oven. Putting the chips in at the last moment will ensure that they don't all end up at the bottom of the sponge. You can also use white chocolate chips to mix things up, if you like.

A 'red velvet' is essentially a cocoa-based, cream-cheese-frosted American delight. The actual red velvet part is the red food colouring that is used to give the cupcake base its gorgeous, rich colour. When you go through the ingredients for this recipe, don't be afraid of the white wine vinegar. Just keep to the quantities and you won't even know it's there, but it's vital to ensure that this rich, dark cupcake stays light as a feather.

Red Velvet Cupcakes

MAKES
12 cupcakes

EQUIPMENT
12-hole muffin tin
12 muffin cases
Freestanding electric mixer
Mixing bowl
Spatula
Teaspoon
Ice cream scoop, size 16
Wire rack
Medium piping bag and large star piping nozzle
  or palette knife

FOR THE CAKES
60g unsalted butter, at room temperature
150g caster sugar
1 egg, at room temperature
20g cocoa powder, sifted
2 tbsp red food colouring
150g plain flour
140ml buttermilk
2¼ tsp baking powder
4½ tsp white wine vinegar

FOR THE FROSTING
40g unsalted butter, at room temperature
100g full-fat cream cheese
250g icing sugar, sifted

FOR THE LOVE (OPTIONAL)
Pink heart-shaped edible sprinkles
Sugar-paste roses and leaves
  (see pages 81 and 141)
Silver edible glitter

To make the cakes
- Preheat the oven to 180°C/350°F/Gas Mark 4 and line the holes of the muffin tin with muffin cases.
- Add the butter and caster sugar to the electric mixer and cream together for 7 minutes, or until light and fluffy.
- Add the egg and mix for 1 minute.
- Mix the cocoa powder and food colouring together with a teaspoon in a separate bowl to make a paste, and then add to the mixer and mix until incorporated. Add the flour and buttermilk and mix for 2 minutes, and then add the baking powder and vinegar and mix for a further 2 minutes.
- Use the ice cream scoop to divide the mixture evenly between the muffin cases. Bake for 25 minutes.
- Remove the baked cupcakes from the oven and immediately transfer to a wire rack. Leave to cool.

To make the frosting
- Cream the butter and cream cheese together in the mixer for 2 minutes.
- Add the icing sugar and beat for about 2 minutes until smooth. Watch closely, as the frosting must remain firm if you are going to pipe it. Chill in the refrigerator until ready to use.

To add the love
- Top the cupcakes with the frosting, either by piping or spreading with a palette knife (see page 51).
- If you like, scatter the frosting with pink heart-shaped edible sprinkles and add sugar-paste roses and leaves. Sprinkle with silver edible glitter.

Love Tip
Using cream cheese here is a wonderful way to prevent the cake from becoming a full-on chocolate explosion if you have less of a sweet tooth. I sometimes like dusting a very little high-quality cocoa powder on top, as it both looks beautiful and cuts through the sharpness of the cream cheese perfectly.

Oreo® Cupcakes

You never know when and how a happy accident will become your inspiration. On a trip to New York I discovered my new best friend, the Oreo biscuit. I stocked up with them on my return, only to discover that they have a nasty knack of falling to the bottom of the shopping bag. This has obvious consequences. So, with those crushed Oreo biscuits we came up with this…

MAKES
12 cupcakes

EQUIPMENT
12-hole muffin tin
12 muffin cases
Freestanding electric mixer
Mixing bowl
Spatula
Ice cream scoop, size 16
Wire rack
Plastic bag
Rolling pin
Tablespoon
Medium piping bag and large star piping nozzle
or palette knife

FOR THE CAKES
60g unsalted butter, at room temperature
150g caster sugar
1 egg, at room temperature
20g cocoa powder, sifted
150g plain flour
140ml buttermilk
2¼ tsp baking powder
4½ tsp white wine vinegar

FOR THE FROSTING
2 Oreo® biscuits
40g unsalted butter, at room temperature
85g full-fat cream cheese
250g icing sugar, sifted

FOR THE LOVE
6 Oreo® biscuits
Sugar-paste leaves (see pages 81 and 141) and small
toy models, or sugar-paste flowers (optional)

To make the cakes
• Preheat the oven to 180°C/350°F/Gas Mark 4 and line the holes of the muffin tin with muffin cases.
• Add the butter and caster sugar to the electric mixer and cream together for 7 minutes, or until light and fluffy.
• Add the egg and mix for 1 minute.
• Add the cocoa powder and mix for 2 minutes, and then add the flour and buttermilk and mix for 2 minutes. Add the baking powder and the vinegar and mix for a further 2 minutes.
• Use the ice cream scoop to divide the mixture evenly between the muffin cases. Bake for 25 minutes.
• Remove the baked cupcakes from the oven and immediately transfer to a wire rack. Leave to cool.

To make the frosting
• Place the biscuits in a plastic bag and seal, making sure that there is no air in the bag. Crush with a rolling pin until you have fine biscuit crumbs.
• Cream the butter and cream cheese together in the mixer for 2 minutes.
• Add the icing sugar and beat until smooth. Watch closely, as the frosting must remain firm if you are going to pipe it. Use a tablespoon to fold in the biscuit crumbs. Chill in the refrigerator until ready to use.

To add the love
• Top the cupcakes with the frosting, either by piping or spreading with a palette knife (see page 51).
• Decorate each cupcake with half an Oreo® biscuit.
• If you like, add a sugar-paste leaf and a small toy model or a couple of sugar-paste flowers.

Love Tip
You can use crushed bourbon biscuits in the frosting instead of Oreos® and top with an extra bourbon. If you are feeling really naughty and don't have a spoon to hand, why not use the bourbon to dunk in the frosting? Who says you can't have your cake (and biscuit) and eat it!

Love Cake
for
Breakfast

The inspiration for these cupcakes came straight from my customers at the Bakery. We open our doors at 10am sharp and it never ceases to amaze me how busy we get first thing with people buying a single cake and a cup of coffee for the journey into work or on the way back from the school run. Cake for breakfast is undeniably a treat (just ask my kids!), but I wanted to create some recipes that celebrated all the good things about a healthy breakfast like cereals, homemade preserves and natural yogurt, and yet looked and tasted just as delicious as our naughtier cupcakes. Of course, you can then legitimately indulge in a chocolate or a red velvet for afternoon tea!

Mocha
Cupcakes

One shot or two…? The trick here lies in the strength of the coffee in the frosting – the darker and stronger it is, the better. This is perfectly finished with an extra flourish in the form of a chocolate-coated coffee bean and, if you want to be totally faithful to your coffee shop favourite, a light dusting of cocoa powder.

MAKES
12 cupcakes

EQUIPMENT
12-hole muffin tin
12 muffin cases
Freestanding electric mixer
Mixing bowl
Spatula
Ice cream scoop, size 16
Wire rack
Microwave oven or heatproof bowl and saucepan
Baking sheet lined with greaseproof paper
Medium piping bag and large star piping nozzle
  or palette knife

FOR THE CAKES
60g unsalted butter, at room temperature
150g caster sugar
1 tsp chicory and coffee extract
1 egg, at room temperature
20g cocoa powder, sifted
150g plain flour
140ml buttermilk
½ tsp bicarbonate of soda
1½ tsp white wine vinegar

FOR THE FROSTING
125g unsalted butter, at room temperature
300g icing sugar, sifted
3 tbsp strong espresso coffee, cooled

FOR THE LOVE
12 chocolate biscuit fingers
12 chocolate-coated coffee beans
Sugar-paste leaves (see pages 81 and 141)
  (optional)
Sifted cocoa powder, for dusting (optional)

To make the cakes
- Preheat the oven to 180°C/350°F/Gas Mark 4 and line the holes of the muffin tin with muffin cases.
- Add the butter, caster sugar and chicory and coffee extract to the electric mixer and cream together for 7 minutes, or until light and fluffy.
- Add the egg and mix for 1 minute.
- Add the cocoa powder and stir in by hand, then mix with the mixer for 1 minute. Add the flour and buttermilk and mix for 2 minutes, and then add the bicarbonate of soda and vinegar and mix for a further minute.
- Use the ice cream scoop to divide the mixture evenly between the muffin cases. Bake for 25 minutes.
- Remove the baked cupcakes from the oven and immediately transfer to a wire rack. Leave to cool.

To make the frosting
- Cream the butter and icing sugar together in the mixer for 2 minutes.
- Add the cooled coffee and mix until well blended.

To add the love
- Top the cupcakes with the frosting, either by piping or spreading with a palette knife (see page 51).
- Decorate each with a chocolate biscuit finger, broken in half, and a chocolate-coated coffee bean.
- Add a sugar-paste leaf and dust with cocoa powder, if you like.

Love Tip
You can buy chocolate-coated coffee beans from most good coffee shops and specialist chocolatiers.

Greek Yogurt & Honey Cupcakes

Let's face it, who doesn't want cake for breakfast. But can yogurt really be its ideal bedfellow? Trust me on this one – it took us a couple of trial runs to get this right at the Bakery, but you'll be glad to know we've cracked it! These cupcakes are our equivalent of warm muffins straight from the oven, and they travel well too if you are rushing out of the door. I've eaten my fair share of these in the car on the school run, as have my kids I'm ashamed to say...

MAKES
12 cupcakes

EQUIPMENT
12-hole muffin tin
12 muffin cases
Freestanding electric mixer
Mixing bowl
Spatula
Ice cream scoop, size 16
Wire rack
Medium piping bag and large star piping nozzle
  or palette knife
Teaspoon

FOR THE CAKES
125g unsalted butter, at room temperature
125g caster sugar
1½ tsp vanilla extract
2 tbsp clear honey
2 eggs, at room temperature
125g self-raising flour
½ tsp baking powder
3 tbsp semi-skimmed milk

FOR THE FROSTING
50g unsalted butter, at room temperature
6 tbsp Greek yogurt
1 tsp lemon juice
380g icing sugar, sifted

FOR THE LOVE
85g best-quality strawberry jam

To make the cakes

- Preheat the oven to 180°C/350°F/Gas Mark 4 and line the holes of the muffin tin with muffin cases.
- Add the butter, caster sugar, vanilla extract and honey to the electric mixer and cream together for 7 minutes, or until light and fluffy.
- Add the eggs, one by one, and mix for 2 minutes.
- Mix the flour and baking powder together in a separate bowl, then add to the mixer and mix until incorporated. Add the milk and mix for a further minute.
- Use the ice cream scoop to divide the mixture evenly between the muffin cases. Bake for 25 minutes.
- Remove the baked cupcakes from the oven and immediately transfer to a wire rack. Leave to cool.

To make the frosting

- Cream the butter, yogurt and lemon juice together in the mixer for 2 minutes until light and fluffy.
- Add the icing sugar, a tablespoonful at a time, mixing after each addition until completely smooth. Chill in the refrigerator until ready to use.

To add the love

- Top the cupcakes with the frosting, either by piping or spreading with a palette knife (see page 51), and then add a teaspoonful of the jam to each.

Love Tip

You can flavour the yogurt however you like. For example, using a fruit compote such as blueberry will give it a delicious antioxidant boost, or you can sprinkle the frosting with some toasted oats or pumpkin seeds.

Apple Cinnamon
Cupcakes

If you're bored with your usual Danish, I think I can help you aspire to something better. These cupcakes are so cheeringly hearty and warming – perfect for a cold winter's morning and perhaps best appreciated while stamping your feet at a freezing bus stop. Both apple and cinnamon are such big, robust flavours that you can add toasted nuts, granola or even some stewed apple to the top of this cupcake and it will hold them really well. And you won't be hungry until lunchtime, I promise… so you see, cake for breakfast is good for you!

MAKES
12 cupcakes

EQUIPMENT
12-hole muffin tin
12 muffin cases
Freestanding electric mixer
Mixing bowls
Zester or grater
Spatula
Ice cream scoop, size 16
Wire rack
Medium piping bag and large star piping nozzle
  or palette knife
Small, sharp knife

FOR THE CAKES
125g unsalted butter, at room temperature
140g caster sugar
2 eggs, at room temperature
200g self-raising flour
1 tsp baking powder
3 tbsp semi-skimmed milk
2 apples, peeled, cored and grated
2 tsp ground cinnamon
½ tsp grated lemon zest

FOR THE FROSTING
125g unsalted butter, at room temperature
300g icing sugar, sifted
1 tbsp semi-skimmed milk
2 tbsp clear honey
¼ tsp ground cinnamon

FOR THE LOVE
1 small apple
Lemon juice, for dipping the apple slices
60g sultanas

To make the cakes
- Preheat the oven to 180°C/350°F/Gas Mark 4 and line the holes of the muffin tin with muffin cases.
- Add the butter and caster sugar to the electric mixer and cream together for 7 minutes, or until light and fluffy.
- Add the eggs, one by one, and mix for 2 minutes.
- Mix the flour and the baking powder together in a separate bowl, then add to the mixer and mix until incorporated. Add milk and mix for a further minute.
- In another bowl, mix the apple, cinnamon and lemon zest together, then add to mixer and mix well.
- Use the ice cream scoop to divide the mixture evenly between the muffin cases. Bake for 25 minutes.
- Remove the baked cupcakes from the oven and immediately transfer to a wire rack. Leave to cool.

To make the frosting
- Cream the butter in the mixer for 2 minutes until light and fluffy.
- Add the icing sugar and milk and mix for a further 2 minutes until well blended, then add the honey and cinnamon and mix well.

To add the love
- Top the cupcakes with the frosting, either by piping or spreading with a palette knife (see page 51).
- Just before serving, cut the apple into slices and then dip in the lemon juice, to avoid discoloration. Decorate each cupcake with 2 apple slices and a few sultanas.

One of the most important things to me when I opened the Love Bakery was that it felt like a place anyone could enjoy, including those that suffer from common allergies. For this reason we don't use nuts in any of the cupcake flavours we create. I also wanted to make cakes for those with an intolerance to gluten – I'm always surprised by the number of people who ask us for gluten-free cakes and I'm thrilled to be able to meet their needs. There's no special alchemy involved, as you can see from this recipe, and if you placed one of these 'special' cupcakes alongside one of our regular cupcakes, you wouldn't be able to tell the difference. So just enjoy!

MAKES
12 cupcakes

EQUIPMENT
12-hole muffin tin
12 muffin cases
Freestanding electric mixer
Mixing bowl
Spatula
Ice cream scoop, size 16
Wire rack
Medium piping bag and large star piping nozzle
    or palette knife

FOR THE CAKES
130g unsalted butter, at room temperature
130g caster sugar
1 tsp vanilla extract
2 eggs, at room temperature
200g gluten-free self-raising flour
4 tbsp semi-skimmed milk

FOR THE FROSTING
125g unsalted butter, at room temperature
½ tsp vanilla extract
250g icing sugar, sifted
1 tbsp semi-skimmed milk

FOR THE LOVE
Silver edible glitter, for sprinkling

To make the cakes
- Preheat the oven to 180°C/350°F/Gas Mark 4 and line the holes of the muffin tin with muffin cases.
- Add the butter, caster sugar and vanilla extract to the electric mixer and cream together for 7 minutes, or until light and fluffy.
- Add the eggs, one by one, and mix for 2 minutes.
- Add the flour to the mixer and mix until incorporated, then add the milk and mix for a further minute.
- Use the ice cream scoop to divide the mixture evenly between the muffin cases. Bake for 25 minutes.
- Remove the baked cupcakes from the oven and immediately transfer to a wire rack. Leave to cool.

To make the frosting
- Cream the butter and vanilla extract together in the mixer for 2 minutes until light and fluffy.
- Add the icing sugar and milk and mix for a further 2 minutes until well blended.

To add the love
- Top the cupcakes with the frosting, either by piping or spreading with a palette knife (see page 51). Sprinkle the frosting with silver edible glitter.

Love Tip
These cupcakes aren't about what you can't have, but enjoying what you can. This same principle can be applied to those who need to limit their sugar intake or stay away from refined sugars. So do your research – there are some excellent sugar substitutes that can be used like for like in place of the sugar in many of the recipes in this book, and look for great-quality chocolate with a high percentage of cocoa solids. Sourcing these ingredients and finding out what tastes good and works well for you is all part of the fun. Love Bakery is all about a little bit of what you fancy does you good!

Gluten-free
Cupcakes

Peruvian Bear
Cupcakes

I've lived all over the world, from Hong Kong to Chicago, but I am – and will always be – a London girl through and through. With the Love Bakery being on the King's Road, Chelsea in the heart of London, what better way to pay homage to our home city than to create a cupcake in honour of one of its most beloved visitors? If you haven't guessed from the title, the giveaway clue here is the marmalade. Oh, and best of luck in matching this cupcake's furry inspiration for polishing off the whole lot in one sitting – you might end up bursting out of your raincoat and galoshes!

MAKES
12 cupcakes

EQUIPMENT
12-hole muffin tin
12 muffin cases
Freestanding electric mixer
Mixing bowl
Spatula
Ice cream scoop, size 16
Wire rack
Apple corer
Medium piping bag and large star piping nozzle
   or palette knife

FOR THE CAKES
60g unsalted butter, at room temperature
150g caster sugar
1 egg, at room temperature
20g cocoa powder, sifted
150g plain flour
140ml buttermilk
½ tsp bicarbonate of soda
1½ tsp white wine vinegar

FOR THE FROSTING
60g unsalted butter, at room temperature
125g icing sugar, sifted
50g cocoa powder, sifted
4 tbsp semi-skimmed milk

FOR THE LOVE
260g (1 tbsp per cupcake) chunky orange
   marmalade
Chopped, candied orange peel, for scattering,
   or red edible dust and bear decorations (optional)

To make the cakes
• Preheat the oven to 180°C/350°F/Gas Mark 4 and line the holes of the muffin tin with muffin cases.
• Add the butter and caster sugar to the electric mixer and cream together for 7 minutes, or until light and fluffy.
• Add the egg and mix for 1 minute.
• Add the cocoa powder and stir in by hand, then mix with the mixer for 1 minute. Add the flour and buttermilk and mix for 2 minutes, and then add the bicarbonate of soda and vinegar and mix for a further minute.
• Use the ice cream scoop to divide the mixture evenly between the muffin cases. Bake for 25 minutes.
• Remove the baked cupcakes from the oven and immediately transfer to a wire rack. Leave to cool.

To make the frosting
• Cream the butter and icing sugar together in the mixer for 2 minutes.
• Add the cocoa powder and mix in by hand, and then add the milk and mix for a further 2 minutes until well blended.

To add the love
• Use the apple corer to remove the centre of each cupcake. Fill with a tablespoon of marmalade, and replace the sponge core (see page 50).
• Top the cupcakes with the frosting, either by piping or spreading with a palette knife (see page 51).
• If you like, scatter the frosting with chopped candied orange peel, or sprinkle wth red edible dust and decorate with edible bear decorations (see template on page 141).

Love Tips
The star of this recipe is the marmalade, and if you want to complement it by giving your frosting an orangey oomph, try mixing in a handful of roughly chopped, candied orange peel – don't worry too much about the exact quantity. For a super-easy Love option, simply top your cupcakes with a dollop of marmalade and finish with a little dusting of icing sugar.

Here, I fold the cream cheese frosting into the sponge mix, along with whole fresh raspberries that soften as the cupcakes bake and then explode in the mouth when bitten into. Try eating these warm from the oven – you don't need to bother frosting them with the sumptuous creamy fruit filling inside the cake. I like to call these cakes my ugly ducklings, since they don't come out as perfectly formed as other cupcakes, but are just as delicious and sweet the way they are!

Raspberry Cream Cheese Cupcakes

MAKES
12 cupcakes

EQUIPMENT
12-hole muffin tin
12 muffin cases
Freestanding electric mixer
Mixing bowl
Spatula
Tablespoon
Ice cream scoop, size 16
Wire rack
Medium piping bag and large star piping nozzle
  or palette knife

FOR THE CAKES
125g unsalted butter, at room temperature
250g caster sugar
½ tsp vanilla extract
200g full-fat cream cheese
2 eggs, at room temperature
300g plain flour
1 tsp baking powder
¼ tsp salt
5 tbsp semi-skimmed milk
4 tbsp raspberry jam

FOR THE LOVE
Sifted icing sugar, for dusting (optional)

To make the cakes
- Preheat the oven to 180°C/350°F/Gas Mark 4 and line the holes of the muffin tin with muffin cases.
- Add the butter, caster sugar, vanilla extract and cream cheese to the electric mixer and cream together for 3 minutes, or until light and fluffy.
- Add the eggs, one by one, and mix for 2 minutes.
- Mix the flour, baking powder and salt together in a separate bowl, then add to the mixer and mix until incorporated. Add the milk and mix for a further minute, and then very gently fold in the jam with a tablespoon.
- Use the ice cream scoop to divide the mixture evenly between the muffin cases. Bake for 30 minutes.
- Remove the baked cupcakes from the oven and immediately transfer to a wire rack. Leave to cool slightly and serve warm, or leave to cool completely.

For the love
- If serving the cupcakes cooled, dust with icing sugar.

Love Tip
For a really decadent summery Sunday brunch version, top the cupcakes with a dollop of whipped fresh cream and decorate with a juicy fresh raspberry.

I'm not sure that I've ever subscribed to the theory that it's difficult to get people to eat healthy fresh fruit, although I do have to say that it's a lot more fun if you can find a way to pair your five a day with a beautifully decorated cupcake!

One of the ways we like to use fruit at Love Bakery is to bake it inside the cake sponge as well as using it to flavour and decorate the frosting. All you do is fold pieces of fresh fruit or berries into your cupcake mixture for a bold fruity experience. Alternatively, simply remove the centre of the cooked cupcake and fill it with luscious fruit jams or preserves, or chopped-up fresh fruit...

Mango Strawberry Cupcakes

It's amazing what you can do with a little imagination, an apple corer and a bowl of fruit that needs to be eaten up. These deliciously original cupcakes contain a surprise at their centre that not only makes them an irresistibly moreish snack but also offers a foolproof way to persuade your kids (large and small!) that they really do love eating healthy fruit.

MAKES
12 cupcakes

EQUIPMENT
12-hole muffin tin
12 muffin cases
Freestanding electric mixer
Mixing bowl
Spatula
Ice cream scoop, size 16
Wire rack
Electric hand whisk
Blender
Apple corer
Medium piping bag and large star piping nozzle
   or palette knife
Small, sharp knife

FOR THE CAKES
125g unsalted butter, at room temperature
150g caster sugar
1½ tsp vanilla extract
2 eggs, at room temperature
175g self-raising flour
½ tsp baking powder
3 tbsp semi-skimmed milk

FOR THE FROSTING
250g mascarpone cheese, chilled
80g icing sugar, sifted

FOR THE LOVE
2 mangoes, peeled and stoned (see Love Tip)
5 strawberries
Finely chopped, skinned pistachio nuts,
   for scattering

To make the cakes
- Preheat the oven to 180°C/350°F/Gas Mark 4 and line the holes of the muffin tin with muffin cases.
- Add the butter, caster sugar and vanilla extract to the electric mixer and cream together for 7 minutes, or until light and fluffy.
- Add the eggs, one by one, and mix for 2 minutes.
- Mix the flour and baking powder together in a separate bowl, then add to the mixer and mix until incorporated. Add the milk and mix for a further minute.
- Use the ice cream scoop to divide the mixture evenly between the muffin cases. Bake for 25 minutes.
- Remove the baked cupcakes from the oven and immediately transfer to a wire rack. Leave to cool.

To make the frosting
- Using the electric hand whisk, whisk the mascarpone and icing sugar together in a large bowl until fairly firm peaks form. Chill in the refrigerator until ready to use.

To add the love
- Add 1 mango and the strawberries to a blender and briefly pulse until you have chunks of fruit, but not a purée.
- Use the apple corer to remove the centre of each cupcake. Fill with the fruit mixture and pack in gently with your finger, then replace the sponge core (see page 50).
- Top the cupcakes with the frosting, either by piping or spreading with a palette knife (see page 51).
- Cut the remaining mango into slices. Top each cupcake with 2 mango slices and scatter with finely chopped pistachio nuts.

Love Tip
To remove the flesh of a mango, place the fruit on a hard surface and, using a sharp knife, cut down either side of the narrow central stone. Take each fleshy piece and score the flesh into cubes with the knife. Push up from the skin side so that the cubes protrude and can be easily sliced off.

Using an apple corer

At Love Bakery we would be lost without our apple corers, and we don't core many apples. Instead we use this handy tool to fill our cupcakes with exciting ingredients, to transform ordinarily lovely sponges into something extraordinary. Apple corers are easy to find in the shops, and are usually included in the kitchen equipment section of supermarkets.

- Place the cooled cupcake on a flat surface.
- Gently push the apple corer into the centre of the cupcake to create a hole. Lift the corer out carefully, remove the sponge trapped inside and put this aside for a moment.
- Using the tip of a knife, fill the hole with jam to the top.
- Place the sponge core gently back into the hole, which locks the jam safely inside the cake.

Fruit fillings

At Love Bakery we sometimes show our love by filling our cupcakes with fresh, ripe fruit. We prepare the fruit using a blender, but you could simply use a fork to chop and mash yours into small chunks. Any left over can be frozen in an ice cube tray. Should you want to add the love at a moment's notice, you can defrost what you need very easily.

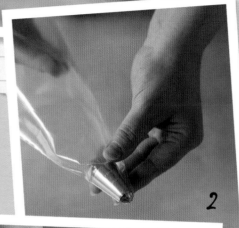

Topping your cakes with frosting

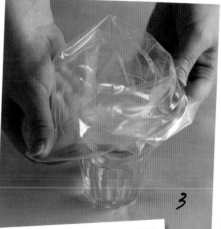

For any of the cupcakes in the book you can happily either pipe on the frosting or simply spread it on, as follows. For piping, you will need a medium piping bag and a large star piping nozzle.

Using a piping bag

- Cut horizontally across the bottom of the piping bag, about 1cm from the tip. Place your nozzle inside the bag to fit into the hole at the tip.
- Place the bag, nozzle down, into a glass tumbler and roll the top of the bag down over the rim of the glass.
- Using a tablespoon, add the frosting to the bag. Two heaped tablespoons of frosting is enough to use at a time. Any more and the bag will be too full and difficult to handle.
- Unroll the bag from the glass rim and remove the bag from the glass. Squeeze the frosting down the bag, then twist the top of the bag so that the frosting is pushed down towards the nozzle.
- Swirl the frosting onto the tops of your cupcakes.

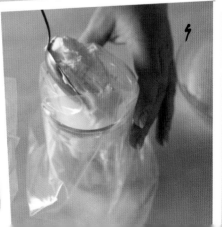

Spreading with a palette knife

Dip a palette knife into the frosting and spread smoothly onto the top of the cupcake. Make sure you add a thick, even layer. Nothing looks worse than a thinly iced cupcake.

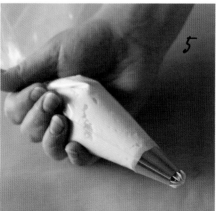

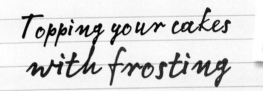

These cupcakes are really popular at the Bakery. In fact, as soon as they are baked, they sell like hot cakes! I guess it's the gorgeous blueberries on top of the cake as well as the little yummy surprise burst of wild blueberry jam in the centre. Everybody knows that blueberries are a superfood, and what more super way could there be to eat them than in a delicious cupcake!

Blueberry Burst Cupcakes

MAKES

12 cupcakes

EQUIPMENT

12-hole muffin tin

12 muffin cases

Freestanding electric mixer

Mixing bowl

Spatula

Ice cream scoop, size 16

Wire rack

Apple corer

Medium piping bag and large star piping nozzle
   or palette knife

FOR THE CAKES

125g unsalted butter, at room temperature

125g caster sugar

1½ tsp vanilla extract

2 eggs, at room temperature

125g self-raising flour

½ tsp baking powder

3 tbsp semi-skimmed milk

FOR THE FROSTING

40g unsalted butter, at room temperature

100g full-fat cream cheese

250g icing sugar, sifted

FOR THE LOVE

260g (1 tbsp per cupcake) wild blueberry jam

125g blueberries

Sifted icing sugar, for dusting

To make the cakes

- Preheat the oven to 180°C/350°F/Gas Mark 4 and line the holes of the muffin tin with muffin cases.
- Add the butter, caster sugar and vanilla extract to the electric mixer and cream together for 7 minutes, or until light and fluffy.
- Add the eggs, one by one, and mix for 2 minutes.
- Mix the flour and baking powder together in a separate bowl, then add to the mixer and mix until incorporated. Add the milk and mix for a further minute.
- Use the ice cream scoop to divide the mixture evenly between the muffin cases. Bake for 25 minutes.
- Remove the baked cupcakes from the oven and immediately transfer to a wire rack. Leave to cool.

To make the frosting

- Cream the butter and cream cheese together in the mixer for 2 minutes.
- Add the icing sugar and beat until smooth. Watch closely, as the frosting must remain firm if you are going to pipe it. Chill in the refrigerator until ready to use.

To add the love

- Use the apple corer to remove the centre of each cupcake. Fill with a tablespoonful of jam and replace the sponge core (see page 50).
- Top the cupcakes with the frosting, either by piping or spreading with a palette knife (see page 51). Decorate each cupcake with 3–5 blueberries and then dust with icing sugar.

Banana Cupcakes

The lovely thing about these cupcakes is the real comfort of nursery food they offer. Make sure that your bananas are completely squishy for this recipe. If I don't have any other fresh ingredients in my kitchen, I can usually rustle up a couple of overripe bananas from the kids' fruit bowl – a situation you may well find familiar!

MAKES

12 cupcakes

EQUIPMENT

12-hole muffin tin
12 muffin cases
Freestanding electric mixer
Mixing bowl
Spatula
Ice cream scoop, size 16
Wire rack
Medium piping bag and large star piping nozzle
   or palette knife

FOR THE CAKES

100g unsalted butter, at room temperature
175g soft light brown sugar
½ tsp banana extract (optional)
2 eggs, at room temperature
300g plain flour
½ tsp baking powder
1 tsp bicarbonate of soda
½ tsp salt
½ tsp ground cinnamon
140ml buttermilk
2 large very ripe bananas, mashed

FOR THE FROSTING

125g unsalted butter, at room temperature
300g icing sugar, sifted
1 tbsp semi-skimmed milk
1 tbsp clear honey

FOR THE LOVE

3 small bananas
12 tsp clear honey

To make the cakes

- Preheat the oven to 180°C/350°F/Gas Mark 4 and line the holes of the muffin tin with muffin cases.
- Add the butter, brown sugar and banana extract, if using, to the electric mixer and cream together for 7 minutes, or until light and fluffy.
- Add the eggs, one by one, and mix for 2 minutes.
- Mix the flour, baking powder, bicarbonate of soda, salt and cinnamon together in a separate bowl, then add to the mixer and mix until incorporated. Add the buttermilk and mashed bananas and mix for a further minute.
- Use the ice cream scoop to divide the mixture evenly between the muffin cases. Bake for 25 minutes.
- Remove the baked cupcakes from the oven and immediately transfer to a wire rack. Leave to cool.

To make the frosting

- Cream the butter in the mixer for 2 minutes until light and fluffy.
- Add the icing sugar, milk and honey and mix for 2 minutes until well blended.

To add the love

- Top the cupcakes with the frosting, either by piping or spreading with a palette knife (see page 51).
- Cut the bananas into thick slices. Decorate each cupcake with 2 banana slices and drizzle with a teaspoonful of honey.

This is my take on the classic rhubarb and custard sweeties that I adored as a kid. The rhubarb offers a wonderfully sharp foil to the sweetness of the cupcake and frosting, but if it's out of season, you can replace it with any other stewing fruit such as apples or pears. In the Bakery we team these up with a custard-flavoured frosting using good old-fashioned canned custard powder, but if you are serving them up at home, why not try them with warm, freshly-made pouring custard?

MAKES
12 cupcakes

EQUIPMENT
12-hole muffin tin
12 muffin cases
Freestanding electric mixer
Mixing bowl
Spatula
Ice cream scoop, size 16
Wire rack
Apple corer
Medium piping bag and large star piping nozzle
    or palette knife

FOR THE CAKES
125g unsalted butter, at room temperature
125g caster sugar
1½ tsp vanilla extract
2 eggs, at room temperature
125g self-raising flour
½ tsp baking powder
3 tbsp semi-skimmed milk

FOR THE FROSTING
125g unsalted butter, at room temperature
½ tsp vanilla extract
250g icing sugar, sifted
2 tbsp shop-bought ready-made custard

FOR THE LOVE
260g (1 tbsp per cupcake) rhubarb jam or stewed
    rhubarb, if in season (see Love Tip)
Sugar-paste flowers (see pages 81 and 141) and
    silver edible glitter, for sprinkling (optional)

To make the cakes
- Preheat the oven to 180°C/350°F/Gas Mark 4 and line the holes of the muffin tin with muffin cases.
- Add the butter, caster sugar and vanilla extract to the electric mixer and cream together for 7 minutes, or until light and fluffy.
- Add the eggs, one by one, and mix for 2 minutes.
- Mix the flour and baking powder together in a separate bowl, then add to the mixer and mix until incorporated. Add the milk and mix for a further minute.
- Use the ice cream scoop to divide the mixture evenly between the muffin cases. Bake for 25 minutes.
- Remove the baked cupcakes from the oven and immediately transfer to a wire rack. Leave to cool.

To make the frosting
- Cream the butter and vanilla extract together in the mixer for 2 minutes until light and fluffy.
- Add the icing sugar and custard and mix for a further 2 minutes until well blended. Chill in the refrigerator until ready to use.

To add the love
- Use the apple corer to remove the centre of each cupcake. Fill with a tablespoonful of the jam or stewed rhubarb and replace the sponge core (see page 50).
- Top the cupcakes with the frosting, either by piping or spreading with a palette knife (see page 51). If you like, decorate with sugar-paste flowers and sprinkle with silver edible glitter.

Love Tip
If you want to use stewed fresh rhubarb instead of jam for the filling, chop 2 rhubarb stalks into small lengths and place in a saucepan with 2 tablespoons water, 1 tablespoon unsalted butter and 2 tablespoons vanilla sugar. Bring to the boil and then simmer for 20 minutes, or until tender. It's now ready to use – don't purée, as it will be too mushy. Any left over is great with pancakes!

Rhubarb &
Custard Cupcakes

Raspberry Coconut Cupcakes

These cupcakes are special favourites of mine. The texture and flavour of the coconut makes them really rich and decadent, but the sharpness of the raspberries prevents them from tasting too over the top. I've frosted them here, but to make them lighter still, you can always just dust with a little icing sugar or add a sprinkling of grated coconut, or top with crème fraîche and a fresh raspberry if you're serving them up right away.

MAKES

12 cupcakes

EQUIPMENT

12-hole muffin tin
12 muffin cases
Freestanding electric mixer
Mixing bowl
Spatula
Ice cream scoop, size 16
Wire rack
Apple corer
Medium piping bag and large star piping nozzle
   or palette knife

FOR THE CAKES

125g unsalted butter, at room temperature
125g caster sugar
1 tsp coconut extract (optional)
2 eggs, at room temperature
125g self-raising flour
½ tsp baking powder
3 tbsp semi-skimmed milk

FOR THE FROSTING

80g unsalted butter, at room temperature
½ tsp coconut extract (optional)
250g icing sugar, sifted
5 tsp coconut milk

FOR THE LOVE

260g (1 tbsp per cupcake) raspberry jam
24 raspberries
100g coconut chips

To make the cakes

- Preheat the oven to 180°C/350°F/Gas Mark 4 and line the holes of the muffin tin with muffin cases.
- Add the butter, caster sugar and coconut extract, if using, to the electric mixer and cream together for 7 minutes, or until light and fluffy.
- Add the eggs, one by one, and mix for 2 minutes.
- Mix the flour and baking powder together in a separate bowl, then add to the mixer and mix until incorporated. Add the milk and mix for a further minute.
- Use the ice cream scoop to divide the mixture evenly between the muffin cases. Bake for 25 minutes.
- Remove the baked cupcakes from the oven and immediately transfer to a wire rack. Leave to cool.

To make the frosting

- Cream the butter and coconut extract, if using, together in the mixer for 2 minutes until light and fluffy.
- Add the icing sugar and coconut milk and mix for a further 2 minutes until well blended. Chill in the refrigerator until ready to use.

To add the love

- Use the apple corer to remove the centre of each cupcake. Fill with a tablespoonful of the jam and replace the core (see page 50).
- Top the cupcakes with the frosting, either by piping or spreading with a palette knife (see page 51). Decorate each cupcake with 2 raspberries and sprinkle with the coconut chips.

Love Tip

Ideally, sprinkle on the coconut chips (available in health food shops) just before serving, otherwise they have a nasty way of absorbing the moisture and you can end up with soggy chips!

Love
Afternoon Tea

I love all the romance and tradition of a high tea and I don't need any excuse to dive into my treasure trove of collected china, mismatched tea plates and novelty teapots, whether I have guests or I'm alone in front of the television with my feet up.

Bring the Love to your teatime by infusing your cupcakes with flavoured teas, presenting Victoria sponge cakes as brightly decorated whoopie pies or playing with the idea of a traditional jam tart, and you can be sure that your tea parties will be anything but stuffy and boring!

Earl Grey Tea
Cupcakes

I'm never especially demanding in life, but the one thing I won't compromise on is a good cuppa, and therein lies the lesson for this cupcake. You must use a good-quality, highly-perfumed tea to make sure that the cupcakes and frosting end up beautifully infused and not bitter. It's worth taking your time to seek out the best tea you can lay your hands on, although if anyone can make it work with a regular cup of builders', can I be the first to know! If you do want to tinker with this recipe, lapsang souchong or orange blossom tea would work just as well.

MAKES

12 cupcakes

EQUIPMENT

12-hole muffin tin
12 muffin cases
Freestanding electric mixer
Mixing bowls
Spatula
Ice cream scoop, size 16
Wire rack
Small, sharp knife
Rolling pin
4cm leaf cutter
Medium piping bag and large star piping nozzle
 or palette knife

FOR THE CAKES

125g unsalted butter, at room temperature
125g caster sugar
2 eggs, at room temperature
125g self-raising flour
½ tsp baking powder
4 tbsp black, strong Earl Grey tea, cooled

FOR THE FROSTING

125g unsalted butter, at room temperature
½ tsp vanilla extract
250g icing sugar, sifted
1 tbsp black, strong Earl Grey tea, cooled

FOR THE LOVE

100g white sugar-paste icing
Mint green, pink and yellow paste food colourings
Silver edible glitter, for sprinkling

To make the cakes

- Preheat the oven to 180°C/350°F/Gas Mark 4 and line the holes of the muffin tin with muffin cases.
- Add the butter and caster sugar to the electric mixer and cream together for 7 minutes, or until light and fluffy.
- Add the eggs, one by one, and mix for 2 minutes.
- Mix the flour and baking powder together in a separate bowl, then add to the mixer and mix until incorporated. Add the tea and mix for a further minute.
- Use the ice cream scoop to divide the mixture evenly between the muffin cases. Bake for 25 minutes.
- Remove the baked cupcakes from the oven and immediately transfer to a wire rack. Leave to cool.

To make the frosting

- Cream the butter and vanilla extract together in the mixer for 2 minutes until light and fluffy.
- Add the icing sugar and tea and mix for a further 2 minutes until well blended.

To add the love

- Divide the sugar-paste icing into 3 and colour one-third with mint green food colouring, another third with pink food colouring and the remaining third with yellow food colouring (see page 81).
- Roll out the 3 icings and use the leaf cutter to cut out approximately 12 leaves from each colour (see page 81). Use the small, sharp knife to mark veins on the leaves.
- Top the cupcakes with the frosting, either by piping or spreading with a palette knife (see page 51), then decorate with the leaves. Sprinkle with silver edible glitter.

These cupcakes exemplify the motto minimum effort, maximum effect – something we love, love, love at Love Bakery! The knack of achieving the eye-catching piped frosting effect here is to fill either side of your piping bag equally with different-coloured frosting.

MAKES
12 cupcakes

EQUIPMENT
12-hole muffin tin
12 muffin cases
Freestanding electric mixer
Mixing bowls
Spatula
Ice cream scoop, size 16
Wire rack
Small, sharp knife
Apple corer
Medium piping bag and large star piping nozzle

FOR THE CAKES
125g unsalted butter, at room temperature
125g caster sugar
1 ½ tsp vanilla extract
2 eggs, at room temperature
125g self-raising flour
½ tsp baking powder
3 tbsp semi-skimmed milk

FOR THE FROSTING
125g unsalted butter, at room temperature
250g icing sugar, sifted
1 tbsp semi-skimmed milk
½ tsp vanilla extract
½ tsp strawberry extract (optional)
Christmas red paste food colouring

FOR THE LOVE
260g (1 tbsp per cupcake) strawberry jam
12 sugar-paste roses (see Love tip on page 20)
Baby pink edible glitter, for sprinkling

To make the cakes
- Preheat the oven to 180°C/350°F/Gas Mark 4 and line the holes of the muffin tin with muffin cases.
- Add the butter, caster sugar and vanilla extract to the electric mixer and cream together for 7 minutes, or until light and fluffy.
- Add the eggs, one by one, and mix for 2 minutes.
- Mix the flour and baking powder together in a separate bowl, then add to the mixer and mix until incorporated. Add the milk and mix for a further minute.
- Use the ice cream scoop to divide the mixture evenly between the muffin cases. Bake for 25 minutes.
- Remove the baked cupcakes from the oven and immediately transfer to a wire rack. Leave to cool.

To make the frosting
- Cream the butter in the mixer for 2 minutes until light and fluffy.
- Add the icing sugar and milk and mix for a further 2 minutes until well blended.
- Divide the frosting in half and spoon into 2 separate bowls. Add the vanilla extract to one bowl and mix well. Add the strawberry extract, if using, to the other bowl. Dip the tip of the small knife into the red food colouring, add to the strawberry frosting and mix well.

To add the love
- Use the apple corer to remove the centre of each cupcake. Fill with a tablespoonful of jam and replace the sponge core (see page 50).
- Place the vanilla frosting down one side of the piping bag fitted with the star nozzle and the pink strawberry frosting down the other side (see Love Tip). Swirl over the tops of the cupcakes. Decorate each with a sugar-paste rose and sprinkle with baby pink edible glitter.

Love Tip
Put your piping bag inside a regular glass tumbler, nozzle downwards, to support it as you fill each side separately (see page 51). That way you avoid frosting scramble, which I guarantee you'll get if you try to hold the bag and fill it at the same time.

Dual-iced
Jam Tart
Cupcakes

CANDY

Gorgeous cupcake holder

I get inspired magpie-ing about in flea markets and junk shops, looking at old photographs or flipping through vintage mags and old catalogues.

Love 'em

Luscious frosting colour

Tea Time Moodboard

Vintage fabrics

pinked edge

English Whoopie Pies

These might sound a bit complicated, but the way we make whoopie pies in the Bakery is by sandwiching together two discs of Victoria sponge with a buttercream frosting. What's great about our whoopies is that they are a wonderful way to update the vintage Victoria sponge, and they hold our handmade sugar decorations beautifully, which we can make as large or small as necessary, depending on the size of the sponges. And after all, who doesn't love a bit of whoopie...

MAKES
6 whoopie pies

EQUIPMENT
Three 4-hole Yorkshire Pudding tins
Freestanding electric mixer
Mixing bowl
Spatula
Tablespoon
Wire rack
Small, sharp knife
2 medium piping bags and 2 large star piping nozzles

FOR THE CAKES
140g unsalted butter, at room temperature,
 plus extra for greasing
140g caster sugar
½ tsp vanilla extract
2 eggs, at room temperature
140g self-raising flour, plus extra for sprinkling
½ tsp baking powder
2 tbsp semi-skimmed milk

FOR THE FROSTING
125g unsalted butter, at room temperature
½ tsp vanilla extract
250g icing sugar, sifted
1 tbsp semi-skimmed milk
Red paste food colouring

FOR THE LOVE
6 sugar-paste decorations, such as butterflies
 (see pages 81 and 141)
Silver and pink edible glitter, for sprinkling

To make the cakes
- Preheat the oven to 170°C/325°F/Gas Mark 3. Grease the holes of the Yorkshire Pudding tins and lightly sprinkle with flour.
- Add the butter, caster sugar and vanilla extract to the electric mixer and cream together for 7 minutes, or until light and fluffy.
- Add the eggs and mix for 1 minute.
- Mix the flour and baking powder together in a separate bowl, then add to the mixer and mix until incorporated. Add the milk and mix for a further minute.
- Use a tablespoon to divide the mixture evenly between the holes of the tins. Bake for 10–12 minutes.
- Remove the baked whoopies from the oven and transfer to a wire rack. Leave to cool.

To make the frosting
- Cream the butter and vanilla extract together in the mixer for 2 minutes until light and fluffy.
- Add the icing sugar and milk and mix for a further 2 minutes until well blended.
- Divide the frosting equally between 2 bowls. Dip the tip of the small knife into red food colouring, add to one bowl and mix well.

- To assemble the Whoopie Pie, see page 70.

Love Tips
For a light, summery alternative to the buttercream frosting, fold some chopped strawberries into fresh whipped cream and use to sandwich the sponges together. Whoopie tins are only available in the United States at the moment through Williams-Sonoma, a speciality gourmet cookware retailer. They are poised to be introduced in the UK in the near future – www.sugarshack.co.uk are working on it.

How to assemble your Whoopie Pies & add the love...

- Taking one frosting colour at a time, put 2 heaped tablespoons of the frosting into one of the piping bags fitted with the large star nozzle (see page 51). Slowly begin to pipe the frosting onto the base of the whoopie.

- Make sure that the layer of frosting isn't too thick. Any thicker than 5cm and you will run out of frosting.

- Place the lid of the whoopie gently onto the lower half.

- With your piping bag, pipe a small amount of frosting on the top half.

- Take a sugar-paste decoration and place it gently into the frosting.

- Take a small knife and dip into a pot of pink edible glitter. Hold it over the whoopie and tap it gently to create an even sprinkling of glitter.

Gift-wrapping Ideas

A beautifully decorated batch of homemade cupcakes is one of the loveliest and most considered gifts you can give. The only downside is that, like flowers, they won't keep forever. The way round this is to present your cupcakes in vintage teacups, or wrapped in a beautiful silk scarf secured with a brooch or in a woven basket lined with hand-picked fabric. Any of these options means that you leave your friends with a gift to treasure long after the cakes have been eaten.

I'm always looking for an excuse to visit my dear friend Margaret at her shop, Vintage Heaven, on London's Columbia Road Flower Market. It's a riot of china, tea caddies, pots and gorgeous fabrics from every period, and I never fail to find something that will complement my baked gifts. More often than not, I find a little something for the shop, too!

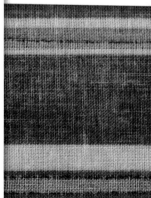

Floaty scarves
in retro colours +
lace trim = instant
individual giftwrap!

Vintage Scrabble
letters that have lost their
board are an inspired
way to label your box of
cupcake delights.

This zingy number is a personal favourite. The luscious lemon curd comes from our lovely friends, Jam Tarts (see page 113). We put it right in the middle so that you get a heavenly surprise when you tuck in, which is then softened by the velvety mascarpone. Each cake is topped with a little daisy. Think breath of fresh air.

Lemon Curd Mascarpone Cupcakes

MAKES
12 cupcakes

EQUIPMENT
12-hole muffin tin
12 muffin cases
Freestanding electric mixer
Zester or grater
Mixing bowl
Spatula
Ice cream scoop, size 16
Wire rack
Electric hand whisk
Apple corer
Rolling pin
Daisy and small circle cutters
Small, sharp knife

FOR THE CAKES
125g unsalted butter, at room temperature
125g caster sugar
1 tbsp grated lemon zest
2 eggs, at room temperature
125g self-raising flour
½ tsp baking powder
3 tbsp semi-skimmed milk

FOR THE FROSTING
250g mascarpone cheese, chilled
100g icing sugar, sifted
150ml double cream

FOR THE LOVE
260g (1 tbsp per cupcake) lemon curd
100g white sugar-paste icing
Yellow paste food colouring
Silver edible glitter, for sprinkling

To make the cakes
- Preheat the oven to 180°C/350°F/Gas Mark 4 and line the holes of the muffin tin with muffin cases.
- Add the butter, caster sugar and lemon zest to the electric mixer and cream together for 7 minutes, or until light and fluffy.
- Add the eggs, one by one, and mix for 2 minutes.
- Mix the flour and baking powder together in a separate bowl, then add to the mixer and mix until incorporated. Add the milk and mix for a further minute.
- Use the ice cream scoop to divide the mixture evenly between the muffin cases. Bake for 25 minutes.
- Remove the baked cupcakes from the oven and immediately transfer to a wire rack. Leave to cool.

To make the frosting
- Cream the mascarpone and icing sugar together in the mixer for 2 minutes until light and fluffy.
- Using the electric hand whisk, beat the cream until thick in a bowl, then add to the mascarpone mixture and mix for a further 2 minutes until well blended. Chill in the refrigerator until ready to use.

To add the love
- Use the apple corer to remove the centre of each cupcake. Fill with a tablespoonful of the lemon curd and replace the core (see page 50).
- Roll out three-quarters of the sugar-paste icing and use the daisy cutter to cut out 12 daisies (see page 81). Use your fingers to curl the petals upwards.
- Colour the remaining sugar paste with yellow food colouring (see page 81) and use the small circle cutter to cut out 12 centres for the daisies. Add to the daisies.
- Top the cupcakes with the frosting, either by piping or spreading with a palette knife (see page 51), then add a daisy and a sprinkling of silver edible glitter to each.

Love Retro

Everyone loves a good fancy-dress party, and as far as I'm concerned there should be nothing serious or at all self-conscious about your baking either. To that end, I've taken some of the best-remembered and most fondly loved retro favourites like **Black Forest Gateau**, **Peach Melba** and even my love of **Disco** and given them the **Love Bakery** treatment. So much fun, so over the top and so delicious! I've also revisited the time-honoured tradition of celebrating the seasons and their festivals to give you a nostalgic collection of cupcakes that capture the essence of those memorable days of spring, summer, autumn and winter.

Boys' Own
Cupcakes

The special ingredient in these cupcakes is marshmallow. My son Henry loves these because you can see the gooey marshmallow inside – an added bonus to an already delicious chocolate cupcake. Get creative with the presentation here. You can obviously buy specialist decorations, but don't be afraid to tailor your cakes to your children's taste with inventive props such as toy soldiers and favourite characters. It goes without saying that you must make sure you don't use toys with small parts, and if you are raiding the toy box, give 'em a good scrub!

MAKES
12 cupcakes

EQUIPMENT
12-hole muffin tin
12 muffin cases
Freestanding electric mixer
Mixing bowl
Spatula
Tablespoon
Ice cream scoop, size 16
Wire rack
Medium piping bag and large star piping nozzle
  or palette knife
7cm-fluted round cutter

FOR THE CAKES
60g unsalted butter, at room temperature
150g caster sugar
1 egg, at room temperature
20g cocoa powder, sifted
150g plain flour
140ml buttermilk
½ tsp bicarbonate of soda
1½ tsp white wine vinegar
12 marshmallows

FOR THE FROSTING
60g unsalted butter, at room temperature
125g icing sugar, sifted
50g cocoa powder, sifted
4 tbsp semi-skimmed milk

FOR THE LOVE
450g white sugar-paste icing
Red and black paste food colourings
Silver edible glitter, for sprinkling

To make the cakes
- Preheat the oven to 180°C/350°F/Gas Mark 4 and line the holes of the muffin tin with muffin cases.
- Add the butter and caster sugar to the electric mixer and cream together for 7 minutes, or until light and fluffy.
- Add the egg and mix for 1 minute.
- Add the cocoa powder and stir in by hand, then mix with the mixer for 1 minute. Add the flour and buttermilk and mix for 2 minutes, and then add the bicarbonate of soda and vinegar and mix for 1 minute.
- Roughly chop the marshmallows into small chunks and fold in with a tablespoon.
- Use the ice cream scoop to divide the mixture evenly between the muffin cases. Bake for 25 minutes.
- Remove the baked cupcakes from the oven and immediately transfer to a wire rack. Leave to cool.

To make the frosting
- Add the butter and icing sugar to the mixer and mix for 2 minutes, then add the cocoa powder and mix in by hand.
- Add the milk and mix for a further 2 minutes until well blended.

To add the love
- Top the cupcakes with the frosting, either by piping or spreading with a palette knife (see page 51).
- Roll out 350g of the white sugar paste thinly and use the fluted round cutter to cut out 12 discs (see page 81).
- Colour half the remaining sugar paste with red food colouring and most of the other half with black food colouring (see page 81), leaving a little white for the robot's features and buttons. Roll out the coloured icings and use the template on page 141 to cut out the robot parts individually and stick together on the discs with a little cooled boiled water. Add the features and buttons as shown.
- Top each cupcake with a robot and sprinkle with silver edible glitter.

Love Tip
If you can get it (look online for suppliers), Marshmallow Fluff® in a jar is a brilliant alternative to frosting for these cakes.

Decoration Ideas

My cupcakes have become known for their distinctive, delicate sugar-paste cut-outs and decorations. This styling is a big part of what we do at the Bakery. I'll confess right here and now, however, that it was a style born out of necessity in the beginning. A pretty sugar butterfly, cut-out heart, stars or edible glitter are easier to apply than you'd think, and they cover any number of mistakes, from sunken cupcakes to icing disasters! The other great thing about these decorations is that as you get more confident about baking and decorating, the only factor that can hold you back is your imagination.

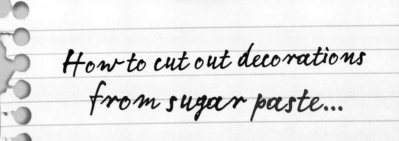

How to cut out decorations
from sugar paste...

Colouring sugar-paste icing

• Put the white sugar-paste icing in a bowl. Dip the tip of a small, sharp knife into the paste food colouring, then place on the edge of the bowl.
• Using your hands, knead the colouring into the icing until it is evenly blended.

Rolling and cutting out

• Roll out the sugar-paste icing on a work surface or chopping board dusted with icing sugar until 5mm thick.
• Cut out shapes from the icing, using either a cutter or a template. You can buy cutters in all shapes and sizes, such as the daisy plunger shown being used below, but we have supplied templates for some of the basic shapes, such as flowers, leaves and butterflies on pages 141.

The nifty idea here is to use mini cupcakes as part of the actual decoration, to construct the Union Jack. But by coordinating the colours, you can create any national flag or design you want. Don't be put off by the large scale of the project or the amount of minis you need to bake – it's simpler than it looks. We suggest you make a slightly smaller version of the flag pictured, using five batches of the cupcakes and frosting given in the recipe (180 cupcakes in total) and frost as instructed. There is a template of the flag on page 141 to help you, which you can scale up if you like.

MAKES
36 mini cupcakes

EQUIPMENT
Two 24-hole mini muffin tins
36 mini muffin cases
Freestanding electric mixer
Mixing bowls
Spatula
Tablespoon
Wire rack
Medium piping bag and large star piping nozzle
Small, sharp knife

FOR THE CAKES
125g unsalted butter, at room temperature
125g caster sugar
1 tsp vanilla extract
2 eggs, at room temperature
150g self-raising flour
½ tsp baking powder
2 tbsp semi-skimmed milk

FOR THE FROSTING
250g unsalted butter, at room temperature
1 tsp vanilla extract
500g icing sugar, sifted
2 tbsp semi-skimmed milk

FOR THE LOVE
Red and blue paste food colourings

To make the cakes
- Preheat the oven to 180°C/350°F/Gas Mark 4 and line the holes of the muffin tins with the mini muffin cases.
- Add the butter, caster sugar and vanilla extract to the electric mixer and cream together for 7 minutes, or until light and fluffy.
- Add the eggs, one by one, and mix for 2 minutes.
- Mix the flour and baking powder together in a separate bowl, then add to the mixer and mix until incorporated. Add the milk and mix for a further minute.
- Use a tablespoon to divide the mixture evenly between the muffin cases. Bake for 15 minutes.
- Remove the baked cupcakes from the oven and immediately transfer to a wire rack. Leave to cool.

To make the frosting
- Cream the butter and vanilla extract together in the mixer for 2 minutes until light and fluffy.
- Add the icing sugar and milk and mix for a further 2 minutes until well blended.

To add the love (one batch)
- Pipe 14 of the cupcakes with the white frosting (see page 51).
- Divide the remaining frosting between 2 bowls: one-third in one bowl, and the remaining two-thirds in the other bowl. Dip the tip of the small knife into blue food colouring, add to the bowl with one-third of the frosting and mix well. Repeat with the red colouring and the bowl with two-thirds of the frosting.
- Pipe 8 cupcakes with the blue frosting and the remaining 14 with the red frosting.
- To assemble the flag shown in the template on page 141, you will need to bake 168 cupcakes (64 red, 68 white and 36 blue). Five batches of this recipe will make 180 cupcakes, leaving you with 12 spare cupcakes – something good to nibble on while you get your flag together.

Love Tips
To give your flag a subtle spangled finish, sprinkle with edible coloured glitter to match the frosting.

Union Jack

Disco
Cupcakes

This is the Studio 54 of cupcakes! It's one of our bestsellers at Love Bakery and you'll be happy to know that it's deceptively simple to create. The cakes are first frosted with buttercream and then decorated randomly with spray food colouring and glitter, graffiti style. It's a great one to get the kids involved with, as you literally can't go wrong – there are no rules here and there's something wonderfully anarchic about spray-painting your cupcakes.

MAKES
12 cupcakes

EQUIPMENT
12-hole muffin tin
12 muffin cases
Freestanding electric mixer
Mixing bowl
Spatula
Ice cream scoop, size 16
Wire rack
Medium piping bag and large star piping nozzle
  or palette knife
Greaseproof paper
Rolling pin
Small star cutter

FOR THE CAKES
125g unsalted butter, at room temperature
125g caster sugar
1½ tsp vanilla extract
2 eggs, at room temperature
125g self-raising flour
½ tsp baking powder
3 tbsp semi-skimmed milk

FOR THE FROSTING
125g unsalted butter, at room temperature
½ tsp vanilla extract
250g icing sugar, sifted
1 tbsp semi-skimmed milk

FOR THE LOVE
Cans of spray food colouring, in colours of
  your choice
100g white sugar-paste icing
Red and blue paste food colourings
Edible glitter, in colours of your choice,
  for sprinkling

To make the cakes
- Preheat the oven to 180°C/350°F/Gas Mark 4 and line the holes of the muffin tin with muffin cases.
- Add the butter, caster sugar and vanilla extract to the electric mixer and cream together for 7 minutes, or until light and fluffy.
- Add the eggs, one by one, and mix for 2 minutes.
- Mix the flour and baking powder together in a separate bowl, then add to the mixer and mix until incorporated. Add the milk and mix for a further minute.
- Use the ice cream scoop to divide the mixture evenly between the muffin cases. Bake for 25 minutes.
- Remove the baked cupcakes from the oven and immediately transfer to a wire rack. Leave to cool.

To make the frosting
- Cream the butter and vanilla extract together in the mixer for 2 minutes until light and fluffy.
- Add the icing sugar and milk and mix for a further 2 minutes until well blended.

To add the love
- Top the cupcakes with the frosting, either by piping or spreading with a palette knife (see page 51).
- Place your iced cupcakes on greaseproof paper. Hold a can of spray food colouring about 7.5cm away and spray to give the desired effect.
- Divide the sugar paste in half and colour one half with red food colouring and the other with blue food colouring (see page 81).
- Roll out the icings and use the star cutter to cut out 12 stars from each colour (see page 81).
- Decorate each cupcake with a red and blue star, then sprinkle with edible glitter.

Love Tip
Serve a frosted but undecorated batch of these cupcakes to your guests before presenting them with a box of cans of spray food colouring and edible glitter and transfers. It might be an idea to put away your best table linen before you all get started...

This is the equivalent of a 1970s dinner party in a cupcake! If you want to go deep retro, try decorating with a whole cherry on the stem – or even a glacé cherry. And if you want to *really* push the boat out, can I suggest using some full-on foil cupcake cases for this one.

MAKES
12 cupcakes

EQUIPMENT
12-hole muffin tin
12 muffin cases
Freestanding electric mixer
Mixing bowl
Spatula
Ice cream scoop, size 16
Wire rack
Apple corer
Medium piping bag and large star piping nozzle
    or palette knife

FOR THE CAKES
60g unsalted butter, at room temperature
150g caster sugar
1 egg, at room temperature
20g cocoa powder, sifted
150g plain flour
140ml buttermilk
½ tsp bicarbonate of soda
1½ tsp white wine vinegar

FOR THE FROSTING
60g unsalted butter, at room temperature
125g icing sugar, sifted
50g cocoa powder, sifted
4 tbsp semi-skimmed milk

FOR THE LOVE
260g (1 tbsp per cupcake) morello cherry jam
100ml double cream, whipped
12 fresh or glacé cherries

To make the cakes
- Preheat the oven to 180°C/350°F/Gas Mark 4 and line the holes of the muffin tin with muffin cases.
- Add the butter and caster sugar to the electric mixer and cream together for 7 minutes, or until light and fluffy.
- Add the egg and mix for 1 minute.
- Add the cocoa powder and stir in by hand, then mix with the mixer for 1 minute. Add the flour and buttermilk and mix for 2 minutes. Then add the bicarbonate of soda and vinegar and mix for a further minute.
- Use the ice cream scoop to divide the mixture evenly between the muffin cases. Bake for 25 minutes.
- Remove the baked cupcakes from the oven and immediately transfer to a wire rack. Leave to cool.

To make the frosting
- Add the butter and icing sugar to the mixer and mix for 2 minutes, then add the cocoa powder and mix in by hand.
- Add the milk to the mixture and mix for a further 2 minutes until well blended.

To add the love
- Use the apple corer to remove the centre of each cupcake. Fill with a tablespoonful of jam and replace the sponge core (see page 50).
- Top the cakes with frosting, either by piping or spreading with a palette knife (see page 51). Pipe a swirl of whipped cream in the middle and place a cherry on top to decorate.

Love Tips
For extra indulgence, why not coat the cherries in chocolate? Melt 100g dark chocolate (minimum 70% cocoa solids) in a microwave oven on Low or in a heatproof bowl set over a saucepan of barely simmering water. Take a cherry by the stem, gently dip into the melted chocolate, and then transfer to a lined baking sheet to set. For cherries without stems, put on a teaspoon and gently lower into the chocolate. Alternatively try soaking some halved fresh cherries in kirsch or schnapps overnight and placing them on top of your cupcakes, or dice and fold them into your frosting if you want to be super retro, super kitsch and super naughty!

Black Forest
Gateau Cupcakes

Violet
Cupcakes

The beauty of making your own cupcakes is that you can tailor their flavour and decoration to the season. Spring, for me, is all about flowers. Love Bakery already loves roses, so here we love-up the delicate violet. The result is not only exquisitely pretty, but defiantly un-shrinking: the crystallized violet petals have a surprisingly strong flavour.

MAKES
12 cupcakes

EQUIPMENT
12-hole muffin tin
12 muffin cases
Freestanding electric mixer
Mixing bowl
Spatula
Ice cream scoop, size 16
Wire rack
Tablespoon
Metal skewer
Medium piping bag and large star piping nozzle
  or palette knife

FOR THE CAKES
60g unsalted butter, at room temperature
150g caster sugar
1 egg, at room temperature
20g cocoa powder, sifted
150g plain flour
140ml buttermilk
½ tsp bicarbonate of soda
1½ tsp white wine vinegar

FOR THE FROSTING
60g unsalted butter, at room temperature
125g icing sugar, sifted
2 tbsp violet syrup or milk
½ tbsp semi-skimmed milk
20g crystallized violet petals, finely crushed,
  plus extra roughly crushed for decoration

FOR THE LOVE
360ml (2 tbsp per cupcake) violet syrup (optional)

To make the cakes
- Preheat the oven to 180°C/350°F/Gas Mark 4 and line the holes of the muffin tin with muffin cases.
- Add the butter and caster sugar to the electric mixer and cream together for 7 minutes, or until light and fluffy.
- Add the egg and mix for 1 minute.
- Add the cocoa powder and stir in by hand, then mix with the mixer for 1 minute. Add the flour and buttermilk and mix for 2 minutes. Then add the bicarbonate of soda and vinegar and mix for a further minute.
- Use the ice cream scoop to divide the mixture evenly between the muffin cases. Bake for 25 minutes.
- Remove the baked cupcakes from the oven and immediately transfer to a wire rack. Leave to cool.

To make the frosting
- Add the butter and icing sugar to the mixer and mix for 2 minutes.
- Add the violet syrup, if using, and milk to the mixture and mix for a further 2 minutes until well blended. Use a tablespoon to fold in the finely crushed crystallized violet petals.

To add the love
- If using the violet syrup, use a skewer to make a few holes in the surface of each cupcake. Very carefully pour 2 tablespoonfuls of violet syrup over the holes in each cupcake.
- Top the cupcakes with the frosting, either by piping or spreading with a palette knife (see page 51). Scatter a few crushed crystallized violet petals over each cupcake.

Again, it's personal, but for me summer evokes memories of my children chomping their way through toffee apples. Love Bakery just had to come up with a cake to capture those warm, sunny, endless days. Children love these yumptious treats. Serve them up at a special tea and you'll be sweetly rewarded by their delighted little faces.

Toffee Apple Cupcakes

MAKES

12 cupcakes

EQUIPMENT

12-hole muffin tin
12 muffin cases
Freestanding electric mixer
Mixing bowls
Spatula
Zester or grater
Ice cream scoop, size 16
Wire rack
Microwave oven or saucepan
Medium piping bag and large star piping nozzle or palette knife

FOR THE CAKES

125g unsalted butter, at room temperature
140g caster sugar
2 eggs, at room temperature
200g self-raising flour
1 tsp baking powder
3 tbsp semi-skimmed milk
2 apples, peeled, cored and grated
½ tsp grated lemon zest
2 tsp ground cinnamon

FOR THE FROSTING

8 chunks fudge, plus extra for decoration
125g unsalted butter, at room temperature
300g icing sugar, sifted
2 tbsp semi-skimmed milk

To make the cakes

- Preheat the oven to 180°C/350°F/Gas Mark 4 and line the holes of the muffin tin with muffin cases.
- Add the butter and caster sugar to the electric mixer and cream together for 7 minutes, or until light and fluffy.
- Add the eggs, one by one, and mix for 2 minutes.
- Mix the flour and baking powder together in a separate bowl, then add to the mixer and mix until incorporated. Add the milk and mix for a further minute.
- In another bowl, mix the apple, lemon zest and cinnamon together, then add to the mixer and mix well.
- Use the ice cream scoop to divide the mixture evenly between the muffin cases. Bake for 25 minutes.
- Remove the baked cupcakes from the oven and immediately transfer to a wire rack. Leave to cool.

To make the frosting

- Melt the fudge in a microwave oven on Low, checking every 10 seconds, or in a saucepan over a low heat to a softened consistency, but be careful not to make it too hot; it just needs to be soft enough to mix with the other ingredients.
- Cream the butter in the mixer for 2 minutes until light and fluffy. Add the icing sugar and milk and mix for a further 2 minutes until well blended. Then add the softened fudge and mix together well.

To add the love

- Top the cupcakes with the frosting, either by piping or spreading with a palette knife (see page 51). Use a couple of pieces of fudge to decorate each cupcake, or if you have any leftover melted fudge, drizzle it over the top and leave to set.

Love Tip

You can buy liquid caramel to use instead of fudge – you will need 3 tablespoons and you won't need to add the milk to the frosting.

Pumpkin Cupcakes

Autumn means only one thing: pumpkins. At Love Bakery we get very, very excited about Halloween. But we're practical as well as over-the-top. What better way of using up the insides of our spooky jack-o-lanterns? For extra spook, add a friendly ghost (toy or sugar paste) and a scary spiderweb cupcake case.

MAKES
12 cupcakes

EQUIPMENT
12-hole muffin tin
12 muffin cases
Freestanding electric mixer
Mixing bowls
Spatula
Ice cream scoop, size 16
Wire rack
Small, sharp knife
Medium piping bag and large star piping nozzle

FOR THE CAKES
120g unsalted butter, at room temperature
250g soft light brown sugar
½ tsp vanilla extract
2 eggs, at room temperature
80g canned pumpkin purée
250g self-raising flour
½ tsp ground cinnamon
½ tsp ground ginger
110ml buttermilk

FOR THE FROSTING
60g unsalted butter, at room temperature
85g full-fat cream cheese
225g icing sugar, sifted
Orange and purple paste food colourings

FOR THE LOVE
12 plastic ghost decorations

To make the cakes
- Preheat the oven to 180°C/350°F/Gas Mark 4 and line the holes of the muffin tin with muffin cases.
- Add the butter, brown sugar and vanilla extract to the electric mixer and cream together for 3–5 minutes, or until light and fluffy.
- Add the eggs, one by one, and mix for 2 minutes, and then add the pumpkin and beat until thoroughly mixed.
- Mix the flour, cinnamon and ginger together in a separate bowl, then add one-third to the mixer and mix until incorporated. Add half the buttermilk and mix again. Repeat until the remaining flour mixture and buttermilk have been incorporated.
- Use the ice cream scoop to divide the mixture evenly between the muffin cases. Bake for 25 minutes.
- Remove the baked cupcakes from the oven and immediately transfer to a wire rack. Leave to cool.

To make the frosting
- Cream the butter and cream cheese together in the mixer for 2 minutes.
- Add the icing sugar and beat until smooth. Watch closely, as the frosting must remain firm if you are going to pipe it.
- Divide the frosting in half and spoon into 2 separate bowls. Dip the tip of the small knife into the orange food colouring, add to one frosting and mix well. Repeat using the purple food colouring.

To add the love
- Place the orange frosting down one side of the piping bag fitted with the star nozzle and the purple frosting down the other side (see page 51). Swirl over the tops of the cupcakes.
- Add a ghost decoration to each cupcake.

Love Tip
I've used canned pumpkin purée in this recipe, but at Halloween you can use the flesh inside your pumpkin lanterns. You'll need 200g, cut into small cubes. Place in a saucepan with 50ml water, bring to the boil and then simmer for 20 minutes until completely soft. Leave to cool, and then transfer, with the water, to a blender and blend to a purée.

Christmas rounds off the year beautifully. For all the staff at Love Bakery, this is a uniquely special time. We love cinnamon and, when the advent calendars are up, we just can't use enough of it. The smell of these cupcakes baking stirs up magical memories, and gets us all loved up about the festive season and new year to come.

Christmas Cupcakes

MAKES
12 cupcakes

EQUIPMENT
12-hole muffin tin
12 muffin cases
Freestanding electric mixer
Mixing bowls
Spatula
Tablespoon
Ice cream scoop, size 16
Wire rack
Medium piping bag and large star nozzle
  or palette knife
Rolling pin

FOR THE CAKES
125g unsalted butter, at room temperature
125g caster sugar
1½ tsp vanilla extract
2 eggs, at room temperature
125g self-raising flour
½ tsp baking powder
1 tsp ground cinnamon
3 tbsp semi-skimmed milk
150g dried cranberries

FOR THE FROSTING
60g unsalted butter, at room temperature
85g full-fat cream cheese
225g icing sugar, sifted
⅛ tsp ground cinnamon
Small pinch of ground cloves

FOR THE LOVE
100g white sugar-paste icing
Green and aqua paste food colourings

To make the cakes
- Preheat the oven to 180°C/350°F/Gas Mark 4 and line the holes of the muffin tin with muffin cases.
- Add the butter, caster sugar and vanilla extract to the electric mixer and cream together for 7 minutes, or until light and fluffy.
- Add the eggs, one by one, and mix for 2 minutes.
- Mix the flour, baking powder and cinnamon together in a separate bowl, then add to the mixer and mix until incorporated. Add the milk and mix for a further minute, then add the cranberries and mix in with a tablespoon.
- Use the ice cream scoop to divide the mixture evenly between the muffin cases. Bake for 25 minutes.
- Remove the baked cupcakes from the oven and immediately transfer to a wire rack. Leave to cool.

To make the frosting
- Cream the butter and cream cheese together in the mixer for 2 minutes.
- Add the icing sugar and beat until smooth. Watch closely, as the frosting must remain firm if you are going to pipe it. Add the cinnamon and cloves and mix to combine. Chill in the refrigerator until ready to use.

To add the love
- Top the cupcakes with the frosting, either by piping or spreading with a palette knife (see page 51).
- Divide the sugar paste into one half and two quarters and colour the half with green food colouring and one-quarter with aqua food colouring (see page 81).
- Roll out the 3 icings and use the templates on page 141 to cut out 24 trees from the green icing, 12 snowflakes from the white icing and 12 snowflakes from the aqua icing.
- Decorate each cupcake with 2 Christmas trees and a white and aqua snowflake.

Peach Melba Cupcakes

Peaches and raspberries are a great combination on their own, but put them in a cake and you have the wow factor. The soft fruit complements the sponge beautifully and the mascarpone frosting makes it super light. This is a cupcake to be enjoyed any time of the year, but especially in the summer when peaches and raspberries are in season.

MAKES
12 cupcakes

EQUIPMENT
12-hole muffin tin
12 muffin cases
Freestanding electric mixer
Mixing bowl
Spatula
Ice cream scoop, size 16
Wire rack
Electric hand whisk
Blender
Apple corer
Medium piping bag and large star piping nozzle
  or palette knife

FOR THE CAKES
125g unsalted butter, at room temperature
150g caster sugar
2 tbsp peach syrup or juice from a can of peaches
2 eggs, at room temperature
175g self-raising flour, sifted
½ tbsp baking powder
3 tbsp semi-skimmed milk

FOR THE FROSTING
250g mascarpone cheese, chilled
80g icing sugar, sifted

FOR THE LOVE
2 peaches, skinned and stoned
A handful of raspberries
6 strawberries, halved

To make the cakes
- Preheat the oven to 180°C/350°F/Gas Mark 4 and line the holes of the muffin tin with muffin cases.
- Add the butter, caster sugar and peach syrup to the electric mixer and cream together for 7 minutes, or until light and fluffy.
- Add the eggs, one by one, and mix for 2 minutes.
- Add the flour, baking powder and milk and mix for 2 minutes.
- Use the ice cream scoop to divide the mixture evenly between the muffin cases. Bake for 25 minutes.
- Remove the baked cupcakes from the oven and immediately transfer to a wire rack. Leave to cool.

To make the frosting
- Using the electric hand whisk, whisk the mascarpone and icing sugar together in a large bowl until fairly firm peaks form. Chill in the refrigerator until ready to use.

To add the love
- Add the peaches and raspberries to a blender and pulse until you have chunks of fruit, but not a purée.
- Use the apple corer to remove the centre of each cupcake. Fill with the fruit mixture and pack in gently with your finger, then replace the core (see page 50).
- Top the cupcakes with the frosting, either by piping or spreading with a palette knife (see page 51).
- Decorate each cupcake with a strawberry half.

This chocolate-based cupcake is a homage to one of my favourite treats when I was a kid. I love to decorate this with some full-on 1980s edible gold leaf and chocolate orange shavings on top.

MAKES
12 cupcakes

EQUIPMENT
12-hole muffin tin
12 muffin cases
Freestanding electric mixer
Zester
Mixing bowl
Spatula
Ice cream scoop, size 16
Wire rack
Electric hand whisk
Blender
Medium piping bag and large star piping nozzle
  or palette knife

FOR THE CAKES
60g unsalted butter, at room temperature
150g caster sugar
1 tbsp grated orange zest
1 egg, at room temperature
20g cocoa powder, sifted
150g plain flour
140ml buttermilk
½ tsp bicarbonate of soda
1½ tsp white wine vinegar

FOR THE FROSTING
60g unsalted butter, at room temperature
125g icing sugar, sifted
50g cocoa powder, sifted
4 tbsp semi-skimmed milk
1 tsp grated orange zest
1–5 drops orange flavouring, to taste

FOR THE LOVE
Twists of orange zest
Sugar-paste flowers (see pages 81 and 141) (optional)

To make the cakes
- Preheat the oven to 180°C/350°F/Gas Mark 4 and line the holes of the muffin tin with muffin cases.
- Add the butter, caster sugar and orange zest to the electric mixer and cream together for 7 minutes, or until light and fluffy.
- Add the egg and mix for 1 minute.
- Add the cocoa powder and stir in by hand, then mix with the mixer for 1 minute. Add the flour and buttermilk and mix for 2 minutes. Then add the bicarbonate of soda and vinegar and mix for a further minute.
- Use the ice cream scoop to divide the mixture evenly between the muffin cases. Bake for 25 minutes.
- Remove the baked cupcakes from the oven and immediately transfer to a wire rack. Leave to cool.

To make the frosting
- Add the butter and icing sugar to the mixer and mix for 2 minutes, then add the cocoa powder and mix in by hand.
- Add the milk and mix with the mixer for a further 2 minutes until well blended. Add the orange zest and flavouring a little at a time, tasting as you do so to make sure that the orange flavour is not too overpowering.

To add the love
- Top the cupcakes with the frosting, either by piping or spreading with a palette knife (see page 51). Decorate each with twists of orange zest and add a sugar-paste flower, if you like.

Love Tip
If you want to make these cupcakes extra special for a dinner party, when cooled, use a skewer to make 3 holes in each cupcake and drizzle over 1 tablespoon Grand Marnier so that it soaks into the sponge. Alternatively, flavour the frosting with 4 tablespoons of Grand Marnier and leave out the milk and orange flavouring, or for a non-alcoholic finishing touch, grate some good old Terry's Chocolate Orange® over the top of each cake.

Love Being
a (big!) Kid

This chapter is for
the kids — whether you
actually are one, or just one at
heart. It's about letting your imagination
run riot and experimenting with all things
crazy, chaotic and fun, like gigantic Donuts,
exploding cupcakes sprinkled with
Popping Candy and Lollipops made out
of cake. The only thing better than baking
these outlandish treats is watching your
guests' expressions when you
serve them up.

Fizzy Whizzy Cupcakes

Serve up these classic vanilla cupcakes with a twist and watch your guests of all ages descend blissfully back into childhood again. The secret is the popping candy – we called it space dust when I was a kid – which is folded into the frosting and explodes in your mouth like tiny firecrackers when you bite into the cake. Not for serious tea parties or the old at heart.

MAKES
12 cupcakes

EQUIPMENT
12-hole muffin tin
12 muffin cases
Freestanding electric mixer
Mixing bowl
Spatula
Ice cream scoop, size 16
Wire rack
Medium piping bag and large star piping nozzle
  or palette knife
Rolling pin
Large and small circle cutters

FOR THE CAKES
125g unsalted butter, at room temperature
125g caster sugar
1½ tsp vanilla extract
2 eggs, at room temperature
125g self-raising flour
½ tsp baking powder
3 tbsp semi-skimmed milk

FOR THE FROSTING
125g unsalted butter, at room temperature
½ tsp vanilla extract
250g icing sugar, sifted
1 tbsp semi-skimmed milk
12 packets popping candy

FOR THE LOVE
100g white sugar-paste icing
Red, cream and black paste food colourings
Silver edible glitter, for sprinkling

To make the cakes
- Preheat the oven to 180°C/350°F/Gas Mark 4 and line the holes of the muffin tin with muffin cases.
- Add the butter, caster sugar and vanilla extract to the electric mixer and cream together for 7 minutes, or until light and fluffy.
- Add the eggs, one by one, and mix for 2 minutes.
- Mix the flour and baking powder together in a separate bowl, then add to the mixer and mix until incorporated. Add the milk and mix for a further minute.
- Use the ice cream scoop to divide the mixture evenly between the muffin cases. Bake for 25 minutes.
- Remove the baked cupcakes from the oven and immediately transfer to a wire rack. Leave to cool.

To make the frosting
- Cream the butter and vanilla extract together in the mixer for 2 minutes until light and fluffy.
- Add the icing sugar and milk and mix for a further 2 minutes until well blended, and then mix in 6 packets of the popping candy.

To add the love
- Top the cupcakes with the frosting, either by piping or spreading with a palette knife (see page 51).
- Divide the sugar paste into 3 and colour one-third with red food colouring, another third with cream food colouring and the remaining third with black food colouring.
- Roll out the 3 icings and use the large and small circle cutters to cut out different-coloured circles from the icings. Use to decorate the cupcakes, and then sprinkle with silver edible glitter. Scatter the remaining 6 packets of popping candy over the top.

Love Tip
Decorate the cupcakes with the popping candy just before serving to ensure that they are still popping when they are eaten. You can find popping candy in most traditional sweet shops.

OK… mistakes *do* happen. Time has a way of drifting on when I am busy baking in the kitchen. So when I left my lovely red velvets in a teeny bit too long they were a little drier than they should be. So it was time to IMPROVISE! After a quick scan of the fridge, out came the cream cheese frosting and, rather than letting it go to waste, my daughter and I started crumbing up the red velvet sponges and mixing them with the frosting. A rummage around in the Just-in-Case Cupboard produced some lolly sticks. Add to the mix a batch of melted chocolate and a lot of sprinkles and ta dah – the Love Pop was born!

MAKES
15-20 Love Pops

EQUIPMENT
12-hole muffin tin
12 muffin cases
Freestanding electric mixer
Mixing bowl
Spatula
Teaspoon
Ice cream scoop, size 16
Wire rack
Tablespoon
Baking sheet lined with greaseproof paper
Microwave oven or heatproof bowl and saucepan

FOR THE CAKES
60g unsalted butter, at room temperature
150g caster sugar
1 egg, at room temperature
20g cocoa powder, sifted
2 tbsp red food colouring
150g plain flour
140ml buttermilk
2¼ tsp baking powder
4½ tsp white wine vinegar

FOR THE FROSTING
20g unsalted butter, at room temperature
40g full-fat cream cheese
125g icing sugar, sifted

FOR THE LOVE
Lolly sticks
800g (coloured) Candy Melts®, or dark chocolate
Edible sprinkles
Sugar-paste flowers and hearts (see pages 81 and 141)

To make the sponge
• Preheat the oven to 180°C/350°F/Gas Mark 4 and line the holes of the muffin tin with muffin cases.
• Add the butter and caster sugar to the electric mixer and cream together for 7 minutes, or until light and fluffy.
• Add the egg and mix for 1 minute.
• Mix the cocoa powder and food colouring together with a teaspoon in a separate bowl to make a paste, and then add to the mixer and mix until incorporated. Add the flour and buttermilk and mix for 2 minutes. Then add the baking powder and vinegar and mix for a further 2 minutes.
• Use the ice cream scoop to divide the mixture evenly between the muffin cases. Bake for 25 minutes.
• Remove the baked cupcakes from the oven and immediately transfer to a wire rack. Leave to cool.

To make the frosting
• Cream the butter and cream cheese together in the mixer for 2 minutes.
• Add the icing sugar and beat until smooth. Chill in the refrigerator until ready to use.

• To assemble the Love Pops, see page 106.

Love
Pops

How to assemble your Love Pops & add the love...

- Break and crumble the cupcakes in a bowl by hand so that you end up with fine crumbs. Add 4 rounded dessertspoonfuls of the frosting.

- Knead the frosting into the sponge to create a firm mixture.

- Shape the mixture into 15–20 balls using the flats of your hands. Add extra frosting if necessary, a little at a time, so that the crumbs and frosting stick together.

- Place the balls on the baking sheet lined with greaseproof paper and chill in the fridge for 3 hours. Take the chilled balls out of the fridge and insert a lolly stick gently into each.

- Melt the different-coloured Candy Melts® separately, or the chocolate, in a microwave oven on High, checking and stirring with a tablespoon every 10 seconds to avoid burning. Alternatively, melt in a heatproof bowl set over a saucepan of simmering water. Dip each chilled ball into the melted candy or chocolate to coat evenly.

- Roll each ball gently in a bowl of edible sprinkles and add sugar-paste flowers and hearts to decorate as you like. Leave to set on a baking sheet.

Love Tip
Wrap your Love Pops individually in cellophane and tie them with a pretty ribbon. If you are giving them as a gift, buy a coloured metal bucket from your local florist and ask them to fill it with oasis. Once you're home, cover the oasis with a pretty piece of coloured netting and place your Love Pops one by one in the oasis for a really nice effect — just like a gorgeous bouquet of flowers!

You Donut

I dreamed this cake up after a friend shouted 'You donut' at another driver for the umpteenth time that day. What started off as a running joke has turned into one of the designs we are famous for at Love Bakery. This cake is a real crowd pleaser – we often have people taking pictures of this donut on a giant scale through the windows of the Bakery whenever we have one on display.

MAKES
1 giant donut

EQUIPMENT
Two 20cm ring mould tins
Freestanding electric mixer
Mixing bowl
Spatula
Tablespoon
Wire rack
Microwave oven or heatproof bowl and saucepan
Palette knife

FOR THE CAKES
250g unsalted butter, at room temperature, plus extra for greasing
300g caster sugar
2 tsp vanilla extract
4 eggs, at room temperature
300g self-raising flour, plus extra for sprinkling
1 tsp baking powder
6 tbsp semi-skimmed milk

FOR THE FROSTING
100g unsalted butter, at room temperature
1 tsp vanilla extract
200g icing sugar, sifted
1 tbsp semi-skimmed milk

FOR THE LOVE
800g (coloured) Candy Melts®, or dark chocolate
Edible sprinkles

To make the cakes

- Preheat the oven to 180°C/350°F/Gas Mark 4. Grease the ring mould tins and lightly sprinkle with flour.
- Add the butter, caster sugar and vanilla extract to the electric mixer and cream together for 7 minutes, or until light and fluffy.
- Add the eggs, one by one, and mix for 2 minutes.
- Mix the flour and baking powder together in a separate bowl, then add to the mixer, a tablespoonful at a time, and mix thoroughly.
- Add the milk, a tablespoonful at a time, and mix well between each addition. Mix for a further 15 seconds.
- Use the tablespoon to divide the mixture evenly between each tin and bake for 25 minutes.
- Remove the cakes from the oven and turn out on to a wire rack. Leave to cool.

To make the frosting

- Cream the butter and vanilla extract together in the mixer for 2 minutes until light and fluffy.
- Add the icing sugar and milk and mix for a further 2 minutes until well blended. Chill in the refrigerator until ready to use.

- To assemble the Donut, see page 110.

Love Tip

You could vary your choice of topping and frosting colour as you like, such as dark chocolate with plain frosting (as pictured here) or pale yellow Candy Melts® and the frosting coloured with pink paste food colouring (see page 111), which makes a dramatic contrast.

How to assemble your Donut & add the love...

- Place one cake flat side up and spoon the frosting onto it.

- Using a palette knife, spread and smooth the frosting over the cake, aiming for an even spread.

- Cover with the other cake, flat side down.

- Melt the Candy Melts® separately, or the chocolate, in a microwave oven on High, checking and stirring with a tablespoon every 10 seconds to avoid burning. Alternatively, melt in a heatproof bowl set over a saucepan of simmering water. Use a tablespoon to spoon the melted candy or chocolate over the donut.

- Scatter edible sprinkles over the top of the donut.

Roger...
(the egg man)

FREE RANGE EGGS

We couldn't do a book about Love Bakery without including Roger the Eggman and his free-range hens. Once a week, every week, Roger delivers the 400 eggs we need for our baking. I'd like to think that he hangs around on delivery days for a gossip and the pleasure of my company, but I have a suspicion that it's down to the cup of tea and cupcake-of-the-day we keep for him! The recipe for this delicious Lemon Curd is dedicated to Roger and his hens. Good-quality, fresh eggs are its key ingredient. I suggest you make it in large batches, as you'll want to keep some in the fridge for later!

Lemon Curd

MAKES
About 650g

INGREDIENTS
Juice and rind of 4 large lemons
100g unsalted butter, diced
350g granulated sugar
4 large eggs

- Grate the rind of the lemons into a heatproof bowl and add the squeezed juice, together with the butter, sugar and eggs.
- Set the bowl over a saucepan of simmering water, making sure that the base isn't touching the water, and stir with a wooden spoon until the butter and sugar are dissolved. Continue stirring constantly until the mixture is thick enough to coat the back of the spoon.
- Pour the curd into warm, sterilized screw-top jars (see page 4) until 'jam packed', screw on the lids tightly and then turn the jars upside down, to ensure an airtight seal.
- Leave until cold and store in the fridge for up to 3 months.

One of the greatest things about Love Bakery is the people I've met along the way as we've been building up the shop. These include mother and daughter Sally Stokes and Annie Hammond who set up their company Jam Tarts, making (and delivering) their own delicious take on homemade jams and preserves using locally sourced organic ingredients. Apart from the fact that their jams help to make our cupcakes taste amazing, they represent all the things we love. This recipe is for their insanely good Strawberry Balsamic jam, which is featured in the Strawberry Daiquiri Cuptails on page 124, and the lemon curd recipe opposite is also their delicious version.

Jam Tarts

Strawberry Balsamic Jam

MAKES
About 3kg

INGREDIENTS
1.5kg strawberries
Juice of 3 lemons
1.5kg granulated cane sugar
5 tbsp balsamic vinegar

- Wash and hull the strawberries and put in a deep preserving pan, crushing a few to release the juice.
- Add the lemon juice and heat gently for 4 minutes.
- Add the sugar and heat, stirring, until it has dissolved.
- Bring to the boil and boil rapidly until setting point is reached: after boiling the jam for about 15 minutes, drop a little onto a chilled plate, put in the fridge for 1 minute, then push with a finger. When it has reached setting point, it will wrinkle.
- Skim off any scum with a metal spoon, remove the pan from the heat and stir in the vinegar.
- Leave to cool slightly, then pour into warm, sterilized screw-top jars (see page 4). Screw on the lids tightly, then turn the jars upside down and leave until the jam is cold and set.
- Store unopened in a cool place for up to a year; transfer to the fridge once opened.

Surprising as it may sound, the first time a customer asked us if we did an actual birthday cake I was stumped – I was just the cupcake lady! I decided that the best way to create a birthday cake the 'Love' way was simply to do what we do best, so with the help of my colleagues at the Bakery we set about figuring out how to bake the biggest cupcake we could fit into our ovens! There's a real 'wow' quality about this cake – when it comes out of the box, the birthday boy or girl (whatever their age) just can't believe the size of the thing; it will feed a dozen people comfortably. If you place the cake on top of a round cake board topped with a sheet of sugar-paste icing, you can personalize it with a name, numbers or a message piped around the edge.

MAKES
1 giant cupcake

EQUIPMENT
Giant cupcake tin
Freestanding electric mixer
Tablespoon
Spatula
Wire rack
Mixing bowls
Small, sharp knife
2 medium piping bags and 2 large star piping nozzles
Rolling pin
Thunderbolt template (see page 141)

FOR THE CAKE
Butter, for greasing
6 eggs, at room temperature, separated
240g caster sugar
5 tbsp vegetable oil
240g self-raising flour, plus extra for sprinkling
½ tsp baking powder
50g cocoa powder, sifted (optional)

FOR THE FROSTING
350g unsalted butter, at room temperature
1½ tsp vanilla extract
700g icing sugar, sifted
8 tbsp semi-skimmed milk

FOR THE LOVE
100g strawberry jam
Red and blue paste food colourings
100g white sugar-paste icing
Silver or black paste food colouring
Edible sprinkles

To make the cake
- Preheat the oven to 180°C/350°F/Gas Mark 4. Grease the cupcake tin and lightly sprinkle with flour.
- Whisk the egg whites in the electric mixer until they form stiff peaks.
- Add the caster sugar and mix for 3–4 minutes, and then add the egg yolks, one by one, and mix after each addition. Add the oil, a tablespoonful at a time, and mix thoroughly.
- Turn the mixer to minimum speed and slowly add the flour, baking powder and cocoa powder, if using. Using a tablespoon, very gently fold the mixture together to avoid knocking out any of the air.
- Divide the mixture equally between the 2 parts of the tin and bake for 40 minutes.
- Remove the cake from the oven and immediately turn out on a wire rack. Leave to cool.

To make the frosting
- Cream the butter and vanilla extract together in the mixer for 2 minutes until light and fluffy.
- Add the icing sugar and milk and mix for a further 2 minutes until well blended.

- To assemble the Giant Cupcake, see page 116.

Love Tip
This outsize cupcake gives you the perfect canvas to go to town with your creative ideas and wow your guests. As an alternative to this dynamic decoration with strong male appeal, you can make it as pretty as you wish by using pink and pastel yellow frosting (see page 117) and adorning it with all the butterflies, flowers and stars you can manage.

The
Giant
Cupcake

How to assemble your Giant Cupcake & add the love...

- Slice the base of the cake in half.

- Take a palette knife and spread a thin layer of strawberry jam on the bottom layer of the cake.

- Use 100g of the frosting to spread on top of the jam.

- Put the upper section of the sponge on top of the base layer. Spread a layer of jam and 100g of frosting on this section.

- Put the domed section on top of the giant cupcake.

- Divide the remaining frosting equally between 2 bowls. Dip the tip of the small knife into red food colouring, add to one bowl and mix well. Repeat with the blue colouring and the other bowl of frosting.

- Fill 2 separate piping bags, each fitted with a large star nozzle with a single colour of frosting. Take the first bag and, working from top to bottom, pipe lines of icing down the side, leaving a gap between each line. Take the second bag of different-coloured icing and pipe lines of icing to fill in the gaps.

- Ice the top of the cupcake in the same way as the side. Begin at the base of the top of the cupcake and ice around the cake (i.e. in a circle rather than top to bottom). This can be iced in one colour, if you prefer.

- Colour the sugar-paste icing with silver or black food colouring, then roll out and use the template on page 141 to cut out some thunderbolts (see page 81). Use to decorate the cake. Finally, scatter over some edible sprinkles!

Chocolate Lime
Grand Prix
Cupcakes

Not only are these cupcakes a divine combination of sweet, rich chocolate cut through with a sharp limey tang, they also fit the 'racing green' theme of this Grand Prix-style cake display to perfection. This scheme makes a fun, inventive alternative to a conventional large single party cake and you can decide how far you want to go with the staging of the 'event' once the cakes themselves are baked and ready to go!

MAKES

12 cupcakes

EQUIPMENT

12-hole muffin tin
12 muffin cases
Freestanding electric mixer
Zester or grater
Mixing bowls
Spatula
Ice cream scoop, size 16
Wire rack
Palette knife
Rolling pin
Small, sharp knife

FOR THE CAKES

60g unsalted butter, at room temperature
150g caster sugar
1 tsp grated lime zest
1 egg, at room temperature
20g cocoa powder, sifted
150g plain flour
140ml buttermilk
½ tsp bicarbonate of soda
1½ tsp white wine vinegar

FOR THE FROSTING

60g unsalted butter, at room temperature
125g icing sugar, sifted
1 tbsp lime extract or juice
3 tbsp semi-skimmed milk
25g cocoa powder, sifted
Green food paste colouring

FOR THE LOVE

100g white sugar-paste icing
Black and mint green paste food colourings

To make the cakes

- Preheat the oven to 180°C/350°F/Gas Mark 4 and line the holes of the muffin tin with muffin cases.
- Add the butter, caster sugar and lime zest to the electric mixer and cream together for 7 minutes, or until light and fluffy.
- Add the egg and mix for 1 minute.
- Add the cocoa powder and stir in by hand, then mix with the mixer for 1 minute. Add the flour and buttermilk and mix for 2 minutes. Then add the bicarbonate of soda and vinegar and mix for a further minute.
- Use the ice cream scoop to divide the mixture evenly between the muffin cases. Bake for 25 minutes.
- Remove the baked cupcakes from the oven and immediately transfer to a wire rack. Leave to cool.

To make the frosting

- Add the butter, icing sugar and lime extract or juice to the mixer and mix for 2 minutes. Add the milk and mix for a further 2 minutes until well blended.
- Divide the frosting in half and spoon into two separate bowls. Add the cocoa powder to one bowl and mix in by hand. Add a little green food colouring to the other bowl and mix well.

To add the love

- Using a palette knife, spread half the cupcakes with the chocolate frosting and the other half with the green frosting (see page 51).
- Colour half the sugar paste with green food colouring and most of the other half with black food colouring, leaving a little white for the dashed lines (see page 81).
- Roll out the coloured icings (see page 81) and cut out strips of varying widths for the tracks as shown. Roll out the white icing and cut out narrow strips. Brush with a little cooled boiled water and attach to the wide black tracks. Position the tracks on the frosted cupcakes.

Love Tip

To top off your cupcakes in winning style, why not add some small plastic racing cars or some car candles?

Love
Cuptails

These cupcakes are strictly for grown-ups. I've taken the classic elements of some of my favourite cocktail recipes and blended them into alcohol-infused delights that are perfect for a girls' night in, a hen night or a sophisticated dinner party. My only advice here is: be careful with the rocket fuel! You can really run riot with these cupcakes, decorating them with sugar-paste olives, classic cocktail umbrellas and candied lemon and lime twists. Manolo Blahniks in the kitchen are an optional extra!

Margarita Cuptails

It's time for a Margarita, Señorita. I dare you to down this tequila-based cupcake in one! Instead of salt on the side, go for a lemon- or lime-soaked sugar crunch topping and don't forget the citrus twist. A word of warning: even though it's got tequila in the frosting, this baby isn't meant for slamming. Not unless you want to repaint the ceiling.

MAKES
12 cupcakes

EQUIPMENT
12-hole muffin tin
12 muffin cases
Freestanding electric mixer
Mixing bowl
Spatula
Ice cream scoop, size 16
Wire rack
Apple corer
Medium piping bag and large star piping nozzle or palette knife
Zester

FOR THE CAKES
125g unsalted butter, at room temperature
125g caster sugar
2 tbsp tequila
2 eggs, at room temperature
125g self-raising flour
½ tsp baking powder
3 tbsp semi-skimmed milk

FOR THE FROSTING
125g unsalted butter, at room temperature
2 tbsp tequila
250g icing sugar, sifted
1 tbsp semi-skimmed milk

FOR THE LOVE
260g (1 tbsp per cupcake) lime jelly
150g coloured sugar
2 limes

To make the cakes
- Preheat the oven to 180°C/350°F/Gas Mark 4 and line the holes of the muffin tin with muffin cases.
- Add the butter, caster sugar and tequila to the electric mixer and cream together for 7 minutes, or until light and fluffy.
- Add the eggs, one by one, and mix for 2 minutes.
- Mix the flour and baking powder together in a separate bowl, then add to the mixer and mix until incorporated. Add the milk and mix for a further minute.
- Use the ice cream scoop to divide the mixture evenly between the muffin cases. Bake for 25 minutes.
- Remove the baked cupcakes from the oven and immediately transfer to a wire rack. Leave to cool.

To make the frosting
- Cream the butter and the tequila together in the mixer for 2 minutes until light and fluffy.
- Add the icing sugar and milk and mix for a further 2 minutes until well blended. Chill in the refrigerator until ready to use.

To add the love
- Use the apple corer to remove the centre of each cupcake. Fill with a tablespoonful of jelly and replace the sponge core (see page 50).
- Top the cupcakes with the frosting, either by piping or spreading with a palette knife (see page 51).
- Place the coloured sugar in a saucer and roll the edge of each cupcake in the sugar to give the effect of frosted glass. Using a zester, pare a lime spiral for each cupcake and add to the cake top.

Rum and ready is the order of the day for this one, my favourite cuptail of all. The lightness of the base and the fresh strawberries make my baked take on a Strawbery Daiquiri the perfect addition to a decadent girlie lunch.

Strawberry Daiquiri Cuptails

MAKES

12 cupcakes

EQUIPMENT

12-hole muffin tin
12 muffin cases
Freestanding electric mixer
Mixing bowls
Spatula
Ice cream scoop, size 16
Wire rack
Electric hand whisk
Zester or grater
Apple corer
Medium piping bag and large star piping nozzle
  or palette knife

FOR THE CAKES

125g unsalted butter, at room temperature
125g caster sugar
1½ tsp strawberry extract (optional)
2 eggs, at room temperature
125g self-raising flour
½ tsp baking powder
3 tbsp semi-skimmed milk

FOR THE FROSTING

250g mascarpone cheese, chilled
100g icing sugar, sifted
100ml double cream
2 tbsp rum
1 tbsp grated lime zest

FOR THE LOVE

260g (1 tbsp per cupcake) strawberry balsamic jam
6 ripe strawberries, halved
12 small mint sprigs

To make the cakes

- Preheat the oven to 180°C/350°F/Gas Mark 4 and line the holes of the muffin tin with muffin cases.
- Add the butter, caster sugar and strawberry extract, if using, to the electric mixer and cream together for 7 minutes, or until light and fluffy.
- Add the eggs, one by one, and mix for 2 minutes.
- Mix the flour and baking powder together in a separate bowl, then add to the mixture and mix until incorporated. Add the milk and mix for a further minute.
- Use the ice cream scoop to divide the mixture evenly between the muffin cases. Bake for 25 minutes.
- Remove the baked cupcakes from the oven and immediately transfer to a wire rack. Leave to cool.

To make the frosting

- Cream the mascarpone and icing sugar together in the mixer for 2 minutes until light and fluffy.
- Using the electric hand whisk, beat the cream until thick in a bowl, then add to the mascarpone mixture and mix for 2 minutes until well blended. Add the rum and lime zest and mix for a few seconds. Chill in the refrigerator until ready to use.

To add the love

- Use the apple corer to remove the centre of each cupcake. Fill with a tablespoonful of jam and replace the sponge core (see page 50).
- Top the cupcakes with the frosting, either by piping or spreading with a palette knife (see page 51).
- Decorate each cupcake with a strawberry half and a small sprig of mint.

Piña Colada Cuptails

If you can't make it to the beach, bake it to the beach! The cupcake version of this most summery of cocktails will add sunshine to any gathering. If your kitsch threshold can withstand it, turn up the love a notch and decorate with a paper umbrella.

MAKES
12 cupcakes

EQUIPMENT
12-hole muffin tin
12 muffin cases
Freestanding electric mixer
Mixing bowl
Spatula
Ice cream scoop, size 16
Wire rack
Medium piping bag and large star piping nozzle or palette knife
Small, sharp knife
Baking sheet

FOR THE CAKES
125g unsalted butter, at room temperature
200g caster sugar
1½ tsp vanilla extract
2 eggs, at room temperature
250g plain flour
2 tsp baking powder
1 tsp salt
100ml pineapple juice
50ml rum
70g desiccated coconut

FOR THE FROSTING
125g unsalted butter, at room temperature
A few drops of coconut extract (optional)
350g icing sugar, sifted
50ml coconut milk

FOR THE LOVE
½ small pineapple (halved lengthways)
2 tbsp clear honey
120g desiccated coconut

To make the cakes
- Preheat the oven to 180°C/350°F/Gas Mark 4 and line the holes of the muffin tin with muffin cases.
- Add the butter, caster sugar and vanilla extract to the electric mixer and cream together for 7 minutes, or until light and fluffy.
- Add the eggs, one by one, and mix for 2 minutes.
- Mix the flour, baking powder and salt together in a separate bowl, then add to the mixer and mix until incorporated. Add the pineapple juice and rum and mix for a further minute, then add the coconut and mix thoroughly.
- Use the ice cream scoop to divide the mixture evenly between the muffin cases. Bake for 25 minutes.
- Remove the baked cupcakes from the oven and immediately transfer to a wire rack. Leave to cool.

To make the frosting
- Cream the butter and the coconut extract, if using, together in the mixer for 2 minutes until light and fluffy.
- Add the icing sugar and coconut milk and mix for a further 2 minutes until well blended.

To add the love
- Top the cupcakes with the frosting, either by piping or spreading with a palette knife (see page 51).
- Remove the core from the pineapple and cut around the skin to remove the flesh. Cut out the 'eyes'. Preheat the grill. Place the pineapple on a baking sheet, drizzle over the honey and grill under a medium heat, turning once, for about 10 minutes, or until caramelized. Leave to cool, then slice into 24 pieces and add 2 to each cupcake. Sprinkle coconut around the pineapple.

Love Tip
It may not be edible, but no piña colada – cuptail or otherwise – is ever complete without a paper umbrella. So make sure you have a store in your just-in-case-cupboard (see page 24); sparklers are optional.

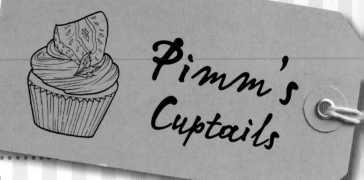

Pimm's Cuptails

Whether your venue is Wimbledon, Lords or a simple picnic in the park, it's cupcake o'clock. Summer suggests exuberance, so you might want to serve these with piles of fresh fruit and a big dollop of vanilla ice cream.

MAKES

12 cupcakes

EQUIPMENT

12-hole muffin tin
12 muffin cases
Freestanding electric mixer
Mixing bowl
Spatula
Ice cream scoop, size 16
Wire rack
Blender
Apple corer
Medium piping bag and large star piping nozzle
   or palette knife

FOR THE CAKES

125g unsalted butter, at room temperature
125g caster sugar
2 tbsp Pimm's No. 1
2 eggs, at room temperature
125g self-raising flour
½ tsp baking powder
3 tbsp semi-skimmed milk

FOR THE FROSTING

125g unsalted butter, at room temperature
1 tbsp Pimm's No. 1
2 drops orange blossom extract (optional)
250g icing sugar, sifted
2 tbsp semi-skimmed milk

FOR THE LOVE

2 strawberries, plus 12 for decoration
5 raspberries, plus 24 for decoration
2 slices peeled orange
2 slices cucumber
A few mint leaves, plus extra for decoration

To make the cakes

- Preheat the oven to 180°C/350°F/Gas Mark 4 and line the holes of the muffin tin with muffin cases.
- Add the butter, caster sugar and Pimm's to the electric mixer and cream together for 7 minutes, or until light and fluffy.
- Add the eggs, one by one, and mix for 2 minutes.
- Mix the flour and baking powder together in a separate bowl, then add to the mixer and mix until incorporated. Add the milk and mix for a further minute.
- Use the ice cream scoop to divide the mixture evenly between the muffin cases. Bake for 25 minutes.
- Remove the baked cupcakes from the oven and immediately transfer to a wire rack. Leave to cool.

To make the frosting

- Cream the butter, Pimm's and orange blossom extract, if using, together in the mixer for 2 minutes until light and fluffy.
- Add the icing sugar and milk and mix for a further 2 minutes until well blended. Chill in the refrigerator until ready to use.

To add the love

- Add the strawberries and raspberries (reserving those for decoration), orange and cucumber slices and mint to the blender and pulse briefly until you have chunks of fruit.
- Use the apple corer to remove the centre of each cupcake. Fill with the fruit mixture and pack in gently with your finger, then replace the sponge core (see page 50).
- Top the cupcakes with the frosting, either by piping or spreading with a palette knife (see page 51).
- Decorate each cupcake with 2 raspberries, a halved strawberry and a few mint leaves.

Whisky Mac Cuptails

A traditional Whisky Mac is an old-fashioned gentleman's drink, and believe me, there's nothing girlie about these cupcakes. The combination of whisky and ginger is beautifully rich and powerful. I love to eat mine with a strong coffee, in my smoking jacket and slippers, in the library, perhaps with a few Labradors around to hoover up any crumbs.

MAKES
12 cupcakes

EQUIPMENT
12-hole muffin tin
12 muffin cases
Freestanding electric mixer
Mixing bowl
Spatula
Ice cream scoop, size 16
Wire rack
Metal skewer
Medium piping bag and large star piping nozzle
   or palette knife

FOR THE CAKES
125g unsalted butter, at room temperature
125g caster sugar
1 tsp ground ginger
1 tsp ground cinnamon
2 eggs, at room temperature
220g plain flour
1½ tsp baking powder
3 tbsp semi-skimmed milk

FOR THE FROSTING
125g unsalted butter, at room temperature
250g icing sugar, sifted
3 tbsp whisky

FOR THE LOVE
4 tbsp whisky
Slices of stem ginger
Demerara sugar, for sprinkling
Edible glitter, for sprinkling

To make the cakes
- Preheat the oven to 180°C/350°F/Gas Mark 4 and line the holes of the muffin tin with muffin cases.
- Add the butter, caster sugar and spices to the electric mixer and cream together for 7 minutes, or until light and fluffy.
- Add the eggs, one by one, and mix for 2 minutes.
- Mix the flour and baking powder together in a separate bowl, then add to the mixer and mix until incorporated. Add the milk and mix for a further minute.
- Use the ice cream scoop to divide the mixture evenly between the muffin cases. Bake for 25 minutes.
- Remove the baked cupcakes from the oven and immediately transfer to a wire rack. Leave to cool.

To make the frosting
- Cream the butter in the mixer for 2 minutes until light and fluffy.
- Add the icing sugar and whisky and mix for a further 2 minutes until well blended. Chill in the refrigerator until ready to use.

To add the love
- Use a skewer to make a few holes in the surface of each cupcake and very carefully pour the whisky over the holes.
- Top the cupcakes with the frosting, either by piping or spreading with a palette knife (see page 51).
- Decorate each cupcake with a few slices of stem ginger and a sprinkling of demerara sugar and edible glitter.

Dessert and drink in one…heavenly! These cuptails are suffused with the delicious richness of Marsala dessert wine. This is what makes the Italian dish on which these cuptails are based such a tiramisu – or pick-me-up –along with espresso coffee. For a decadent touch, try garnishing with strands of golden saffron.

Tiramisu Cuptails

MAKES
12 cupcakes

EQUIPMENT
12-hole muffin tin
12 muffin cases
Freestanding electric mixer
Mixing bowl
Spatula
Ice cream scoop, size 16
Wire rack
Electric hand whisk
Metal skewer
Medium piping bag and large star piping nozzle
  or palette knife
Grater

FOR THE CAKES
125g unsalted butter, at room temperature
125g caster sugar
1½ tsp vanilla extract
2 eggs, at room temperature
125g self-raising flour
½ tsp baking powder
3 tbsp semi-skimmed milk

FOR THE FROSTING
125g mascarpone cheese, chilled
100g icing sugar, sifted
100ml double cream

FOR THE LOVE
100ml strong coffee, cooled
50ml Marsala wine
70g caster sugar
60g cocoa powder
50g dark chocolate, finely grated

To make the cakes
- Preheat the oven to 180°C/350°F/Gas Mark 4 and line the holes of the muffin tin with muffin cases.
- Add the butter, caster sugar and vanilla extract to the electric mixer and cream together for 7 minutes, or until light and fluffy.
- Add the eggs, one by one, and mix for 2 minutes.
- Mix the flour and baking powder together in a separate bowl, then add to the mixer and mix until incorporated. Add the milk and mix for a further minute.
- Use the ice cream scoop to divide the mixture evenly between the muffin cases. Bake for 25 minutes.
- Remove the baked cupcakes from the oven and immediately transfer to a wire rack. Leave to cool.

To make the frosting
- Cream the mascarpone and icing sugar together in the mixer for 2 minutes until light and fluffy.
- Using the electric hand whisk, beat the cream until thick in a bowl, then add to the mascarpone mixture and mix for a further 2 minutes until well blended. Chill in the refrigerator until ready to use.

To add the love
- Mix the coffee, Marsala and caster sugar together. Use a skewer to make a few holes in the surface of each cupcake and very carefully pour the Marsala mixture over the holes.
- Top the cupcakes with the frosting, either by piping or spreading with a palette knife (see page 51).
- Place the cocoa powder in a saucer and roll the cupcake gently in the powder to give a light covering. Add a little finely grated dark chocolate on top.

WALKED

MUST *do something with sequins*

Am POSITIVE have seen Carrie in one of these

French Line
S.S.CHAMPLAIN

45

Am truly 'in love' with 'Choo' straps

LOST

THIS BIG CITY

29

La la Louboutin!

Loving paper leaves!

31   1 INCH   2   3

Party Moodboard

Rebecca Saraceno
&
André Hugo
invite

---

to join them in celebrating
their wedding day on

THURSDAY 2 APRIL 2009
CEREMONY AT 5.30 PM
AND RECEPTION TO FOLLOW AT
CONSTANTIA UITSIG RESTAURANT
CONSTANTIA UITSIG WINE FARM
SPAANSCHEMAT RIVER ROAD
CONSTANTIA
CAPE TOWN
WWW.CONSTANTIA-UITSIG.COM

HOLLYWOOD ROOSEVELT
A HULL HOTEL
Home of the Stars
HOLLYWOOD

HOTEL
LUTETIA
PARIS

Organic
chic

BON VOYAGE

Cosmopolitan Cuptails

High heels and high times! This is Cake in the City time. Cocktails and cuptails with your girlfriends are a lovely way to come together before a night on the tiles. At the Bakery, our sophisticated Cosmopolitans are a firm favourite with hen parties, but it's not essential to get engaged before you sample their deliciousness.

MAKES
12 cupcakes

EQUIPMENT
12-hole muffin tin
12 muffin cases
Freestanding electric mixer
Mixing bowl
Spatula
Ice cream scoop, size 16
Wire rack
Zester or grater
Apple corer
Medium piping bag and large star piping nozzle or palette knife

FOR THE CAKES
125g unsalted butter, at room temperature
125g caster sugar
1½ tsp vanilla extract
2 eggs, at room temperature
125g self-raising flour
½ tsp baking powder
3 tbsp semi-skimmed milk

FOR THE FROSTING
125g unsalted butter, at room temperature
1 tbsp Cointreau
250g icing sugar, sifted
2 tbsp lime juice
1 tbsp grated lime zest

FOR THE LOVE
260g (1 tbsp per cupcake) cranberry jam
140g dried cranberries
12 mint leaves
Silver edible glitter, for sprinkling

To make the cakes
- Preheat the oven to 180°C/350°F/Gas Mark 4 and line the holes of the muffin tin with muffin cases.
- Add the butter, caster sugar and vanilla extract to the electric mixer and cream together for 7 minutes, or until light and fluffy.
- Add the eggs, one by one, and mix for 2 minutes.
- Mix the flour and baking powder together in a separate bowl, then add to the mixer and mix until incorporated. Add the milk and mix for a further minute.
- Use the ice cream scoop to divide the mixture evenly between the muffin cases. Bake for 25 minutes.
- Remove the baked cupcakes from the oven and immediately transfer to a wire rack. Leave to cool.

To make the frosting
- Cream the butter and Cointreau together in the mixer for 2 minutes until light and fluffy.
- Add the icing sugar and lime juice and zest and mix for a further 2 minutes until well blended. Chill in the refrigerator until ready to use.

To add the love
- Use the apple corer to remove the centre of each cupcake. Fill with a tablespoonful of jam, and replace the sponge core (see page 50).
- Top the cupcakes with the frosting, either by piping or spreading with a palette knife (see page 51).
- Decorate each cupcake with a few dried cranberries, a mint leaf and a sprinkling of the glitter.

After Eight – or whenever you fancy. These After Eight® cuptails are a sassy combination of dessert and liqueur. Chocolate and mint are a classic combination that few can resist. If I receive an invitation to dinner, I sometimes give the host a dozen of these cuptails, in a box wrapped with a beautiful ribbon, as a lovely alternative to chocolates or wine.

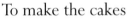

After Eight® Cuptails

MAKES
12 cupcakes

EQUIPMENT
12-hole muffin tin
12 muffin cases
Freestanding electric mixer
Mixing bowl
Spatula
Ice cream scoop, size 16
Wire rack
Medium piping bag and large star piping nozzle

FOR THE CAKES
60g unsalted butter, at room temperature
150g caster sugar
½ tsp mint flavouring
1 egg, at room temperature
20g cocoa powder, sifted
150g plain flour
140ml buttermilk
½ tsp bicarbonate of soda
1½ tsp white wine vinegar

FOR THE FROSTINGS
125g unsalted butter, at room temperature
250g icing sugar, sifted
50g cocoa powder, sifted
2 tbsp semi-skimmed milk
2 tbsp crème de menthe
1–5 drops of mint extract, to taste
1 tsp mint green paste food colouring

FOR THE LOVE
6 After Eight® mints

To make the cakes
- Preheat the oven to 180°C/350°F/Gas Mark 4 and line the holes of the muffin tin with muffin cases.
- Add the butter, caster sugar and mint flavouring to the electric mixer and cream together for 7 minutes, or until light and fluffy.
- Add the egg and mix for 1 minute.
- Add the cocoa powder and stir in by hand, then mix with the mixer for 1 minute. Add the flour and buttermilk and mix for 2 minutes. Then add the bicarbonate of soda and vinegar and mix for a further minute.
- Use the ice cream scoop to divide the mixture evenly between the muffin cases. Bake for 25 minutes.
- Remove the baked cupcakes from the oven and immediately transfer to a wire rack. Leave to cool.

To make the frostings
- For the chocolate frosting, add half the butter and half the icing sugar to the mixer and cream together for 2 minutes, then mix in the cocoa powder by hand. Add one tablespoon of the milk and one tablespoon of the crème de menthe to the mixture and mix for a further 2 minutes until well blended. Cover and set aside.
- Repeat for the mint frosting, using the remaining butter, sugar, milk and crème de menthe. Add the mint extract, a little at a time, to achieve the desired flavour, then the green food colouring.

To add the love
- Place the chocolate frosting down one side of the piping bag fitted with the large star nozzle and the mint frosting down the other side (see page 51). Swirl over the tops of the cupcakes.
- Cut each mint in half to make 2 triangles and decorate each cupcake with one triangle.

Gift tags

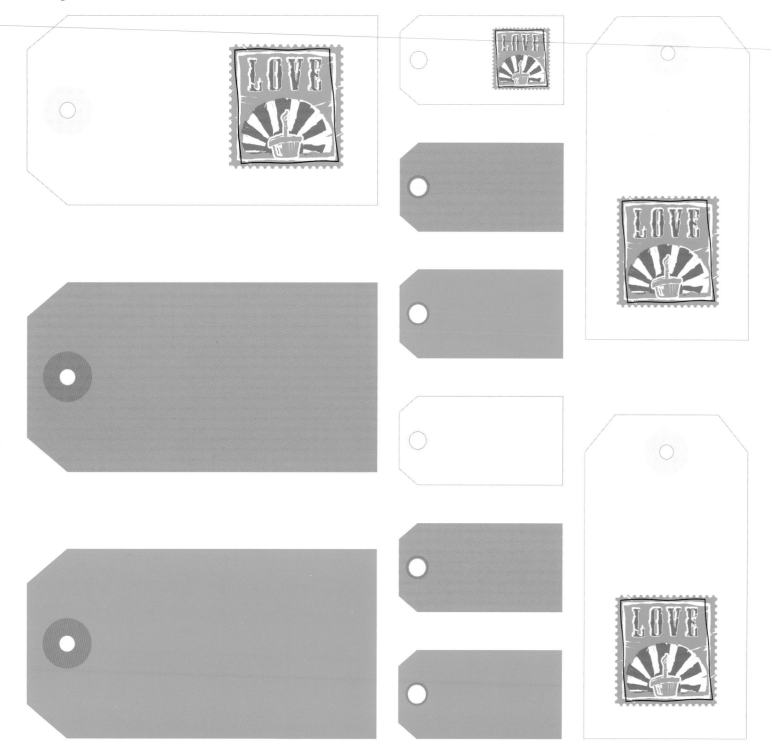

Template for a basic Union Jack Flag (see page 82).

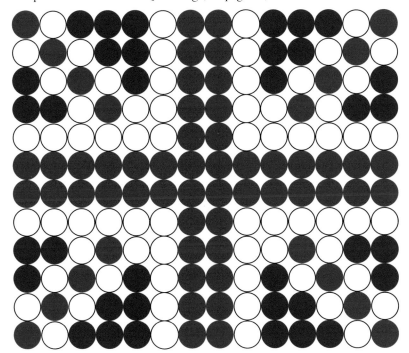

Useful
Templates

Templates for sugar-paste icing decorations.

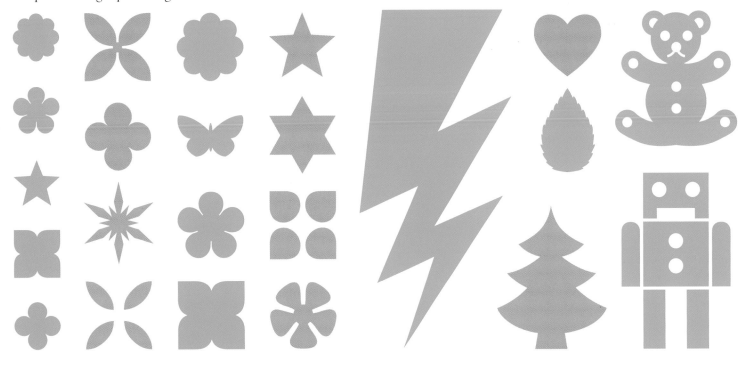

Index

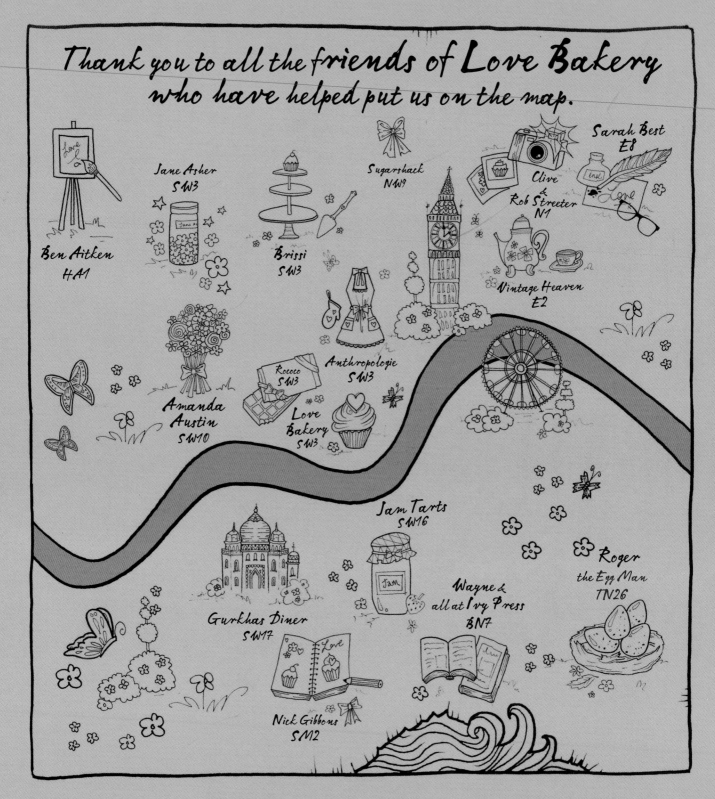